PREFACE

"Fundamentals of Sericulture: A Complete Guide from Mulberry Cultivation to Silk Production"

This comprehensive guide explores the fascinating world of sericulture, covering every aspect from mulberry cultivation to silk production. The book explores silkworm biology, morphology, rearing techniques, and common diseases, beginning with an in-depth look at mulberry varieties, agronomic practices, and disease management. Readers will gain insights into cocoon harvesting, silk reeling, and processing methods, as well as the utilization of sericulture byproducts. The economics and marketing of the sericulture industry are discussed, along with the application of modern technologies and the global silk trade. With its detailed explanations, practical tips, and emphasis on sustainable practices, this book is an invaluable resource for students, researchers, and practitioners interested in the art and science of silk production.

ACKNOWLEDGMENT

I, **Katta Subramanya Sai Teja**, would like to first and foremost express my heartfelt gratitude to my family - my father, mother, and brother (**Mr. Katta Rama Rao, Smt. Katta Kalyani, and Katta Vijay Krishna**) for their unwavering love and understanding throughout this endeavor, and I owe them a great deal of gratitude for assisting me in navigating this life journey and shaping who I am today. I am grateful to **Mr. Deepak Kumar Mahanta**, the most important person in my life, for being my sounding board, cheerleader, and confidant, as well as for his constant belief in me and my goals. I am also grateful to one of my best friends, **Mr. Venkateswarlu**, for his consistent support so far.

I want to offer sincere thanks to all of my teachers, seniors, juniors, and friends who generously assisted me in writing this book. I'd like to thank my team (**Ms. Sujatha G S, Ms. Dharanikota Lalithambica Devi and Mr. Gadde Anil Kumar**) for their valuable time, encouragement, guidance, and listening ear throughout the way to this milestone. Their insights gave me further depth and perspective, and I am grateful for them.

CONTENT

Chapter 1

Introduction to Sericulture

Sericulture is the practice of rearing silkworms for the production of silk. It originated in China over 5000 years ago and has since spread to many countries, with China and India being the top two producers today. Sericulture involves several stages, beginning with the cultivation of mulberry plants, which serve as the primary food source for the silkworms. The leaves of these plants are harvested and fed to the silkworms, which undergo four moults as they grow, shedding their exoskeleton each time.

Once the silkworms have reached maturity, they begin to spin their cocoons using a single continuous thread of raw silk. The cocoons are then harvested, and the silk is extracted through a process called reeling. This involves softening the cocoons in hot water to dissolve the gummy sericin holding the fibres together, and then unwinding the freed filaments onto a reel. The raw silk may then be twisted or plied into yarn and undergoes further processing, such as degumming and dyeing, before being woven into fabric.

Sericulture provides employment and economic benefits to millions of people, particularly in rural areas of developing countries. It is a labour-intensive industry that requires relatively low capital investment, making it well-suited for small-scale farmers. However, sericulture also faces several challenges, such as the susceptibility of silkworms to diseases and pests, as well as competition from synthetic fibres. Despite these challenges, sericulture remains an important and valuable industry, producing a natural, renewable, and biodegradable fibre with unique properties and a rich cultural heritage.

Importance and history of sericulture

Sericulture, the cultivation of silkworms to produce silk, is an important ago-based industry that provides several economic, social and environmental benefits, especially in developing countries. Here are some key points highlighting the importance of sericulture:

Economic Benefits

1. High employment potential: Sericulture is a labour-intensive industry that can generate vast employment opportunities in rural areas. It is used as a tool for rural economic development and reconstruction.

2. Additional income for farmers: Sericulture provides farmers an opportunity to earn additional income alongside their regular farming activities. Silkworm rearing has a short gestation period and provides frequent returns with relatively low investment.

3. Supports rural economies: A significant portion (around 57%) of the income generated from silk production flows back to the rural growers and communities, thus supporting the vitality of villages and rural economies.

Social Benefits

1. Women empowerment: Sericulture is a women-friendly industry. A large proportion of the labour force involved in sericulture, from mulberry cultivation to silk reeling, is women. It provides them income and employment.

2. Inclusive development: Sericulture is well-suited for marginalized communities like the Adivasi tribes in India. It helps in poverty alleviation and prevents migration of rural people to urban areas in search of employment.

Environmental Benefits

1. Eco-friendly: Sericulture is largely an eco-friendly activity. Mulberry cultivation helps in soil conservation and erosion prevention. Silkworm rearing does not generate pollution or emit greenhouse gases.

2. Biodegradable and renewable: Silk is a natural, biodegradable and renewable fibre, unlike many synthetic fibres which have a larger environmental footprint.

3. Efficient land use: Sericulture can be practiced efficiently on small land holdings. The mulberry plants can be grown on land not suitable for other crops.

Other Benefits

1. Supports other industries: Sericulture supports many other industries like weaving, textile, handicrafts etc. Silk is a high

value product with a strong demand in both domestic and export markets.

2. Byproducts utilization: Apart from silk, there are several useful byproducts from sericulture. Mulberry fruits are nutritious, silkworm pupae are used in cosmetics and pharmaceuticals, and silkworm litter is used for biogas production.

Sericulture is a sustainable agro-industry with immense potential for generating employment, supporting rural development, empowering women and conserving the environment. With the growing demand for silk and natural fibers, sericulture is poised to play an increasingly important role in the years to come, especially in developing economies.

Overview of the sericulture industry and its future prospects

Sericulture is the process of cultivating silkworms to produce silk. It involves several stages:

1. Moriculture - cultivation of mulberry plants to feed silkworms

2. Silkworm rearing - hatching silkworm eggs and feeding larvae with mulberry leaves until they are ready to spin cocoons

3. Cocoon harvesting - collecting the spun cocoons and sorting them by quality

4. Silk reeling and processing - extracting raw silk filament from cocoons and processing it into silk yarn and fabric

Sericulture is an important agro-based cottage industry, especially in developing countries like China and India which are the top two silk producers globally. It provides employment to millions of people, particularly women, in rural areas. India is the only country that produces all five commercial silks - mulberry, tropical tasar, oak tasar, eri and muga silk.

In 2020-21, India produced 33,739 MT of raw silk, with mulberry silk accounting for 70.72%, tasar 8.02%, eri 20.55% and muga 0.71%. The silk production declined by 5.8% compared to 2019-20 due to disruptions caused by the Covid-19 pandemic. The export earnings in 2020-21 were Rs. 1418.97 crores.

Future Prospects of Sericulture Industry

The sericulture industry has good potential for growth in the coming years:

- Increasing demand for silk: There is a growing demand for superior quality silk, especially bivoltine silk, in the domestic and export markets for value-added products. The government is providing technical and financial assistance to enhance bivoltine silk production.

1. **Employment generation:** Sericulture can generate substantial employment in rural areas as it is labour-intensive with low capital investment. It is estimated to employ around 8.7 million people in India currently.

2. Women empowerment: Sericulture is a women-friendly industry as it involves mostly indoor activities that are less physically demanding. It can provide income and employment to rural women.

3. Sustainable production: Sericulture has a low environmental impact as mulberry cultivation helps in soil conservation. Silk is a natural, biodegradable and renewable fibre unlike synthetic fibres.

4. Byproduct utilization: Apart from silk, there is potential to commercially utilize sericulture byproducts like silkworm pupae, sericin, silk waste etc. for pharmaceutical, food and animal feed applications.

5. Technological innovations: Adoption of new technologies in sericulture like IoT sensors for real-time monitoring, solar-powered equipment, biotechnology tools to enhance silkworm breeds etc. can improve productivity and quality.

However, the industry also faces some challenges like silkworm diseases, weather fluctuations, shortage of skilled labour, competition from synthetic fibres etc. which need to be addressed.

The sericulture industry has bright prospects as a sustainable means of generating employment, empowering rural communities, especially women, and producing a valuable natural textile - silk. With growing demand and technological upgradation, sericulture can continue to play an important role in the rural economy of developing countries.

Chapter 2

Moriculture (Mulberry Cultivation)

Mulberry varieties and their characteristics

Variety	Key Characteristics
S-1635	-Triploid variety with high leaf yield - Suitable for irrigated conditions - Planting through saplings at 60 cm x 60 cm spacing - Performs well throughout India - Leaf yield of 50-55 MT/ha/year
S-146	-Belongs to Morus alba - White fruits, native to China - Suitable for wide range of climatic conditions - Leaf yield of 35-40 MT/ha/year
S36	- High yielding variety - Leaf yield of 40-45 MT/ha/year - Nutritive leaves essential for good growth of silkworm larvae - Suitable for irrigated conditions in South India
MR2	- Developed by TN Sericulture Dept, Coonoor in 1970 - Resistant to powdery mildew disease - Popular in plains of Tamil Nadu - Leaf yield of 25-30 MT/ha/year - Susceptible to thrips attack

Kanva-2 (M5)	- Hybrid of Mysore local variety - Leaf yield of 25-30 MT/ha/year - Does not grow well in rainfed areas - Suitable for irrigated conditions in South India
Tr-10	- Also called Natikaddi - Cultivated in traditional sericultural tracts of Karnataka - Low yielding variety - Leaf yield around 8 MT/ha/year in rainfed and 25 MT/ha/year in irrigated conditions
S-140 (PPR-1)	- Superior leaf quality - High leaf moisture content and moisture retention capacity - High total soluble carbohydrates, proteins and chlorophyll content
Vishala	- High leaf yield variety - Leaf yield of 45-50 MT/ha/year - Suitable for irrigated conditions
RC1, MSG2, AGB8	- Tropical mulberry varieties developed through classical breeding - High foliage yield of 40-45 MT/ha/year - Drought tolerant - Resistant to major pests and diseases
S-13	- Belongs to Morus indica - Selection from open-pollinated hybrids of Kanva-2 - Leaf yield of 8-12 MT/ha/year under rainfed conditions

	- Resistant to leaf spot and powdery mildew
S-34	- Belongs to Morus indica - Selection from progeny of S30 x Berc 776 - Leaf yield of 15 MT/ha/year under rainfed conditions - Resistant to powdery mildew and leaf rust
Ichinose	- Imported from Japan - High leaf quality - Suitable for wide range of climatic conditions
Kokuso-27	- Imported from Japan - High leaf quality - Suitable for wide range of climatic conditions

Cultivation practices

Planting

Mulberry trees can be planted as bare-root or container-grown trees in late winter or early spring before new growth begins. They prefer full sun locations with well-draining, loamy soil. Dig a planting hole that is 2-3 times wider than the root ball and the same depth. Loosen the soil at the bottom of the hole. Position the tree so the top of the root ball is level with the surrounding soil. Backfill with the native soil, firming it around the roots to eliminate air pockets. Water deeply after planting.

Spacing depends on the variety and intended use. For orchards, space trees 15-30 feet apart. For hedgerows or living fences, plant 4-6 feet apart. Dwarf varieties can be spaced 6-10 feet apart.

Pruning

Mulberries don't require extensive pruning. The main goals are to develop a strong framework when the tree is young and to remove dead, diseased or crossing branches as needed.

For young trees, select 3-4 strong, evenly spaced branches to be the main scaffold limbs. Remove or head back competing branches. As the tree grows, remove branches that grow downward, rub against each other, or are overcrowded.

Mature trees benefit from occasional thinning to allow light into the canopy. This stimulates new growth and increases fruit production. Prune lightly after harvest or during dormancy in winter. Avoid heavy pruning which can lead to bleeding.

Mulberries can also be pruned into single-stemmed trees, multi-stemmed bushes, or even hedges depending on the landscaping needs.

Fertilization

Mulberries generally don't require heavy fertilization. Applying a balanced, slow-release fertilizer in early spring is usually sufficient. Use a formula like 10-10-10 at a rate of about 1 pound per 1" of trunk diameter.

Organic options like well-rotted manure, compost, or blood meal can also be used. Apply a 2–3-inch layer of organic material as a mulch around the tree, keeping it a few inches away from the trunk.

Avoid over-fertilizing, especially with nitrogen, as this can lead to excessive vegetative growth at the expense of fruit production.

Irrigation

While somewhat drought-tolerant once established, mulberries benefit from consistent moisture, especially during fruit development. Provide 1-2 inches of water per week, adjusting for rainfall. Deep, infrequent irrigation is better than frequent, shallow watering.

Mulching with organic materials helps retain soil moisture and moderate soil temperatures. Apply a 3–4-inch layer, keeping it a few inches away from the trunk to prevent rot.

Harvesting

- Leaf harvesting starts 6-8 months after planting when the plants attain a height of 1.5-1.75 m.

- The first harvest is done by bottom pruning at 15-30 cm above ground level.

- Subsequent harvests are taken at 60-70 day intervals by shoot harvesting method, retaining 1-2 mature leaves on the shoot.

- 5-6 harvests can be taken per year depending on the growth.

- Expected leaf yield is 15-20 MT/ha in the first year and 30-60 MT/ha from 2nd year onwards under irrigated conditions.

Diseases and pests of mulberry plants

Mulberry plants are susceptible to various diseases and pests that can significantly impact their growth, yield, and the quality of leaves, which are essential for silkworm rearing in sericulture.

Fungal Diseases

1. Leaf Spot

- Caused by fungi such as *Cercospora moricola*, *Cercosporella mori*, and *Pseudocercospora mori*

- Symptoms: Small, circular to irregular, brown spots on leaves that may coalesce to form larger patches; severe infections lead to premature defoliation

- Management: Pruning infected leaves, maintaining proper spacing, and applying fungicides like Carbendazim or Hexaconazole

2. Powdery Mildew

- Caused by the fungus *Phyllactinia corylea*

- Symptoms: White, powdery growth on leaf surfaces, leading to yellowing and premature leaf fall

- Management: Maintaining proper spacing, pruning infected leaves, and applying fungicides like Carbendazim or Hexaconazole

3. Root Rot

- Caused by fungi such as *Fusarium solani*, *Fusarium oxysporum*, and *Macrophomina phaseolina*

- Symptoms: Wilting, yellowing of leaves, rotting of roots, and eventual death of the plant

- Management: Removing and burning infected plants, applying neem cake, and using antagonistic fungi like *Trichoderma viride*

4. Stem Canker

- Caused by the fungus *Botryodiplodia theobromae*

- Symptoms: Greyish-brown discoloration of bark, delayed sprouting, death of buds and sprouts, and black eruptions on the bark

- Management: Avoiding planting during winter months, pre-treating cuttings with Carbendazim, and dressing cut surfaces after pruning

Bacterial Diseases

1. Bacterial Blight

- Caused by the bacterium ***Pseudomonas syringae pv. mori***

- Symptoms: Water-soaked spots on leaves, curling and rotting of leaves, and black lesions on young shoots

- Management: Pruning infected parts, avoiding overhead irrigation, and applying copper-based bactericides or antibiotics like Streptomycin

Viral Diseases

1. Mulberry Mosaic

- Caused by the Mulberry mosaic virus (MMV)

- Symptoms: Mosaic patterns, mottling, and chlorosis on leaves, leading to reduced leaf size and quality

- Management: Removing and burning infected plants, using disease-free planting material, and controlling insect vectors

Nematode Diseases

1. Root Knot

- Caused by the nematode ***Meloidogyne incognita***

- Symptoms: Formation of galls or knots on roots, stunted growth, yellowing of leaves, and wilting

- Management: Deep ploughing during summer, applying neem cake, and using nematicides like Carbofuran

Pests

Sap Suckers

1. Mealy Bugs (*Maconellicoccus hirsutus* and *Paracoccus marginatus*)

- Symptoms: Curling, crinkling, and twisting of leaves; stunted growth; and honeydew secretion leading to sooty mold growth

- Management: Pruning infested parts, releasing predators like ***Cryptolaemus montrouzieri***, and applying neem oil or insecticides like DDVP

2. Thrips (*Pseudodendrothrips mori*)

- Symptoms: Silvery streaks and brown edges on leaves, curling and crinkling of leaves, and premature leaf fall

- Management: Installing yellow sticky traps, releasing predators like ***Chrysoperla*** (green lacewing), and applying neem oil or insecticides like DDVP

3. Jassids (*Empoasca flavescens*)

- Symptoms: Yellowing and curling of leaves, stunted growth, and reduced leaf yield

- Management: Pruning infested parts, maintaining proper spacing, and applying neem oil or insecticides like DDVP

4. Whiteflies (*Dialeuropora decempuncta*)

- Symptoms: Yellowing and wilting of leaves, honeydew secretion leading to sooty mold growth, and reduced leaf yield

- Management: Installing yellow sticky traps, maintaining proper spacing, and applying neem oil or insecticides like DDVP

Defoliators

1. Bihar Hairy Caterpillar (*Spilosoma obliqua*)

- Symptoms: Skeletonization of leaves, complete defoliation in severe cases, and presence of hairy caterpillars

- Management: Hand-picking and destroying caterpillars and egg masses, releasing parasitoids like *Apanteles spp.*, and applying insecticides like DDVP

2. Leaf Roller (*Diaphania pulverulentalis*)

- Symptoms: Rolling and webbing of leaves, feeding on green tissues, and presence of larval frass

- Management: Pruning and destroying infested leaves, installing light traps, and applying insecticides like DDVP

3. Wingless Grasshopper (*Neorthacris acuticeps*)

- Symptoms: Feeding on leaves, buds, and green bark, leading to defoliation and stunted growth

- Management: Deep ploughing during summer, maintaining weed-free conditions, and applying insecticides like DDVP

Borers

1. Stem Borer (*Apriona cinerea*)

- Symptoms: Presence of larval tunnels in stems, wilting and drying of branches, and sawdust-like frass near the base of the plant

- Management: Pruning and burning infested branches, inserting wire into larval tunnels to kill the larvae, and applying insecticides like Chlorpyrifos

Effective management of mulberry diseases and pests involves a combination of cultural practices, biological control agents, and judicious use of chemical pesticides. Regularly monitoring mulberry plantations, maintaining proper sanitation, and adopting integrated pest management (IPM) strategies can help minimize the impact of these biotic stressors on mulberry growth and leaf quality.

Chapter 3

Silkworm Biology

Silkworm morphology, anatomy and physiology

Morphology

Here are the key morphological characteristics of the silkworm, *Bombyx mori*, at its different life stages:

Egg:

- Small, round to slightly oval shape

- About 1 mm in diameter

- Pale yellow when freshly laid, gradually turning gray as the embryo develops

- Covered by a hard, protective shell called the chorion

Larva (Caterpillar):

- Cylindrical body divided into head, thorax and abdomen

- Newly hatched larva is about 2-3 mm long with black, hairy appearance

- Mature 5th instar larva grows up to 5-8 cm long

- Smooth, white body with a prominent horn-like structure on the last abdominal segment

- Head has simple eyes (stemmata), short antennae, and powerful chewing mouthparts

- Thorax has 3 pairs of jointed, clawed true legs

- Abdomen has 5 pairs of unjointed prolegs with crochets

- Body covered with fine setae arising from tubercles in a specific pattern that differs among strains

Pupa:

- Obtect type, 2-3 cm long

- Ovoid shape, brown colour

- Enclosed in a silk cocoon

- Appendages like antennae, legs and wing pads fused to the body

- Segmentation of abdomen visible

- Cremaster present at the posterior tip for anchoring inside the cocoon

Adult (Moth):

- Stout, hairy body, about 2.5 cm long

- Pale white to creamy colour with faint brown stripes

- Females larger than males

- Head with large, feather-like antennae; males have broader antennae than females

- Vestigial, non-functional mouthparts

- Two pairs of broad, rounded wings covered with minute scales

- Wings have reduced venation and are incapable of flight

- Legs short and hairy

- Abdomen large, especially in females which are heavy with eggs

- External genitalia present at the tip of abdomen

The silkworm shows distinct morphological features adapted for its specific lifestyle at each stage of its life cycle, from the tiny eggs to the worm-like feeding larva, the quiescent pupa inside the cocoon, and finally the flightless adult moth specialized for reproduction. The morphology also reflects the impact of domestication and selective breeding over thousands of years.

Biology

Silkworms, the larval form of the domesticated silk moth *Bombyx mori*, are holometabolous insects that undergo complete metamorphosis through four distinct life stages: egg, larva, pupa, and adult. Each stage has unique morphological characteristics adapted for specific functions.

Egg Stage

The life cycle begins with the egg stage. Silkworm eggs are small, round, and slightly flattened, with a diameter of about 1 mm. Freshly laid eggs are light yellow but gradually darken to gray as the embryo develops. The eggshell, or chorion, is hard and protects the developing embryo from environmental stresses.

Larval Stage

After hatching, silkworms enter the larval stage, which is the only feeding stage. Newly hatched larvae, or first instars, are about 2-3 mm long and have a black, hairy appearance. As they feed on mulberry leaves and grow, silkworms moult four times, shedding their exoskeleton and entering the next larval instar. With each moult, the larva's size increases, and its appearance changes.

The fifth and final instar larva, also called the mature silkworm, is about 5-8 cm long and has a smooth, white appearance with a prominent horn-like structure on the last abdominal segment. The larva has a well-developed digestive system adapted for efficiently converting mulberry leaves into silk proteins.

The silkworm's body is divided into three main parts: head, thorax, and abdomen. The head bears the mouthparts, antennae, and simple eyes (stemmata). The thorax has three pairs of jointed legs, while the abdomen has five pairs of fleshy prolegs with crochets for gripping surfaces.

Pupal Stage

At the end of the larval stage, the mature silkworm stops feeding and begins to spin a cocoon for the pupal stage. The pupa, formed inside the cocoon, is an immobile, non-feeding stage during which the larval tissues are broken down and reorganized into the adult structures.

The silkworm pupa is brown, oval-shaped, and about 2-3 cm long. It has a hard, protective exoskeleton and a prominent cremaster at the posterior end for anchoring inside the cocoon.

Adult Stage

The adult silkworm, or silk moth, emerges from the cocoon after about 2-3 weeks of pupal development. The moth has a heavy body, a pair of large, feathery antennae, and vestigial mouthparts, as it does not feed during its short adult life span of about a week.

The female moth is larger than the male, with a swollen abdomen full of eggs. The male moth has a more slender abdomen and larger, bushier antennae for detecting the female's pheromones. Both sexes have two pairs of wings covered with fine scales, but they are unable to fly due to their large, heavy bodies and reduced wing venation.

The primary function of the adult stage is reproduction. After mating, the female moth lays 300-500 eggs, completing the life cycle.

Throughout its life cycle, the silkworm undergoes remarkable morphological changes adapted for its specific lifestyle and silk production. Understanding these morphological characteristics is essential for optimizing silkworm rearing and silk production in sericulture.

Physiology

Anatomy of the Digestive System

The alimentary canal of the silkworm larva is a straight tube divided into three main regions: the foregut (stomodaeum), midgut (mesenteron), and hindgut (proctodaeum).

1. Foregut

- Consists of the mouth, pharynx, oesophagus, and a small crop

- Lined with a cuticular intima and has squamous epithelial cells with small nuclei

- Responsible for ingestion and passage of food to the midgut

2. Midgut

- Largest part of the alimentary canal, forming a simple tube

- Lined with a single layer of columnar epithelial cells and interspersed with goblet cells

- Columnar cells have a brush border of microvilli on the apical surface for absorption

- Goblet cells secrete mucus to lubricate the gut and protect the epithelium

- Primary site of digestion and absorption of nutrients

- Divided into anterior, middle, and posterior regions with functional differentiation

- Peritrophic membrane encloses the food bolus, compartmentalizing digestion

3. Hindgut

- Consists of the ileum, colon, rectum, and anus

- Lined with a cuticular intima and has polygonal epithelial cells with large nuclei

- Responsible for water and ion reabsorption and elimination of faecal matter

- Malpighian tubules, the excretory organs, open at the junction of midgut and hindgut

Physiology of Digestion

1. Ingestion and Digestion

- Silkworm larvae feed voraciously on mulberry leaves during the larval stages

- Leaves are masticated by the mandibles and mixed with saliva containing digestive enzymes

- Food passes through the foregut to the midgut where major digestion occurs

- Midgut lumen has an alkaline pH ranging from 8.0 to 10.5, optimal for digestive enzymes

- Midgut secretes various enzymes such as amylases, proteases, lipases, and cellulases

- Digestion is both extracellular in the lumen and intracellular in the columnar cells

2. Absorption and Nutrient Distribution

- Nutrients are absorbed by the columnar cells through microvilli

- Absorbed nutrients are transported to the hemolymph for distribution to tissues

- Iron absorption and distribution in the midgut show functional differentiation

- Anterior midgut absorbs more iron than posterior regions

3. Elimination of Waste

- Undigested food residue passes from the midgut to the hindgut

- Water and ions are reabsorbed in the hindgut to conserve resources

- Faecal matter is eliminated through the anus as small pellets

Developmental Changes

- The digestive system undergoes remodelling during metamorphosis

- During the prepupal stage, the larval gut degenerates through programmed cell death

- Autophagy and apoptosis are involved in the destruction of the larval gut cells

- Larval gut is replaced by the adult gut during pupal development

- Adult moth has a vestigial digestive system as it does not feed

The digestive system of the silkworm larva is well-adapted for efficient digestion and absorption of nutrients from mulberry leaves. The functional differentiation of the midgut and the coordinated action of digestive enzymes enable the rapid growth and development of the silkworm during the larval stages. Understanding the structure and physiology of the silkworm digestive system is crucial for optimizing silkworm rearing and silk production in sericulture.

Circulatory System

The silkworm has an open circulatory system, where the blood or hemolymph flows freely through the body cavity or hemocoel, bathing the internal organs directly. The hemolymph is a clear, colorless fluid that contains hemocytes (blood cells), nutrients, wastes, and signalling molecules. It plays a vital role in transporting nutrients, removing metabolic wastes, and mediating immune responses.

Hemolymph Composition

The haemolymph of B. mori consists of a liquid plasma in which hemocytes are suspended. The plasma contains various organic and inorganic components:

- Proteins: These include storage proteins like 30K proteins, lipophorins, and vitellogenins, as well as immune-related proteins like phenoloxidase and antimicrobial peptides.

- Amino acids: Free amino acids are abundant in the hemolymph, with glutamine, histidine, and lysine being the most prominent. These serve as nutrient reserves and osmoregulators.

- Carbohydrates: Glucose, fructose, and trehalose are the main sugars found in the hemolymph. Trehalose, a disaccharide, is the primary blood sugar in insects.

- Lipids: Diacylglycerols and phospholipids are present in the hemolymph, often associated with lipophorins for transport.

- Inorganic ions: The hemolymph contains various ions like Na^+, K^+, Ca^{2+}, Mg^{2+}, Cl^-, and phosphates that help maintain osmotic balance and pH.

Hemocytes

Hemocytes are the cellular components of the hemolymph. In B. mori, five main types of hemocytes have been identified:

1. Prohemocytes: These are small, round cells with a high nucleus to cytoplasm ratio. They are considered to be the stem cells that differentiate into other hemocyte types.

2. Plasmatocytes: These are the most abundant hemocytes. They are oval or spindle-shaped cells involved in phagocytosis, encapsulation, and wound healing.

3. Granulocytes: These are round or oval cells with cytoplasmic granules. They participate in phagocytosis, encapsulation, and melanization reactions.

4. Spherulocytes: These cells contain large, refractile spherules in their cytoplasm. Their function is not well understood, but they may be involved in transport and storage of cuticular components.

5. Oenocytoids: These are large, round cells that synthesize phenoloxidase, an enzyme crucial for melanization reactions in the immune response.

Hemolymph Circulation

The circulation of hemolymph in B. mori is driven by a tubular, segmented heart called the dorsal vessel that runs along the dorsal midline of the body. The dorsal vessel is divided into the heart proper in the abdomen and the aorta in the thorax.

The heart consists of 8 chambers, each with a pair of lateral openings called ostia. Hemolymph enters the heart through the ostia during diastole and is pumped forward by peristaltic contractions of the heart muscles. The hemolymph then flows out of the aorta into the head and bathes the tissues of the head and thorax.

From the thorax, the hemolymph moves posteriorly through the hemocoel, passing through the narrow pericardial sinus surrounding the heart. It then re-enters the heart through the ostia, completing the circulatory cycle.

Accessory pulsatile organs, called the ventral diaphragm and the caudal pulsatile organ, help circulate the hemolymph in the appendages and the posterior abdomen, respectively.

Physiological Functions

The hemolymph serves several vital physiological functions in B. mori:

1. Nutrient transport: It carries nutrients like amino acids, sugars, and lipids from the gut and fat body to various tissues for growth and metabolism.

2. Waste removal: Metabolic wastes are removed from the tissues and transported to the excretory organs (Malpighian tubules) for elimination.

3. Hormone distribution: Hormones like ecdysteroids and juvenile hormone are distributed throughout the body via the hemolymph to regulate development and metamorphosis.

4. Immune defense: Hemocytes and humoral factors in the hemolymph work together to combat pathogens and parasites through phagocytosis, encapsulation, and melanization.

5. Thermoregulation: The hemolymph helps distribute heat evenly throughout the body and plays a role in regulating body temperature.

6. Hydrostatic skeleton: The hemolymph acts as a hydrostatic skeleton, providing support and facilitating movement by hydraulic pressure.

The open circulatory system of B. mori, with its hemolymph and hemocytes, plays a central role in maintaining homeostasis, supporting growth and development, and defending against pathogens. Understanding the composition and functions of the hemolymph is crucial for optimizing silkworm rearing and silk production in sericulture.

Respiratory System

Structure of the Respiratory System

The silkworm has an open respiratory system consisting of a network of tubes called tracheae that deliver oxygen directly to the tissues. The main components are:

1. Spiracles

  - Paired openings on the lateral sides of the thorax and abdomen

  - 9 pairs in total - 1 pair on the prothorax, 1 pair on the metathorax, and 7 pairs on the first seven abdominal segments

- Each spiracle has a valve-like structure to regulate airflow and minimize water loss

2. Tracheae

- Tubular extensions that arise from the spiracles and branch into progressively smaller tubes

- Larger tracheae have spiral thickenings called taenidia which prevent collapse

- Smaller tracheae lack taenidia and are called tracheoles

- Tracheoles are less than 1 μm in diameter and terminate inside cells, sometimes forming extensive networks on the surface of highly metabolic tissues like muscles

3. Air sacs

- Dilated portions of the tracheae that serve as air reservoirs

- Lack taenidia and can collapse and expand to aid in ventilation

- Found in the thorax and abdomen, especially in actively flying adult moths

Mechanism of Respiration

1. Diffusion

- Primary mode of gas exchange, especially in smaller larvae and pupae

- Oxygen diffuses from the spiracles through the tracheae and tracheoles into the cells

- Carbon dioxide diffuses out in the opposite direction

- Occurs passively along concentration gradients without requiring active ventilation

2. Ventilation

- Becomes important in larger, more active stages like late instar larvae and adult moths

- Achieved by rhythmic contraction and relaxation of abdominal muscles

- Compression of air sacs in the abdomen pushes air forward through the tracheae

- Spiracular valves open and close in coordination with abdominal movements

- Unidirectional airflow from posterior to anterior spiracles improves efficiency of gas exchange

Developmental Changes

- First instar larvae have only two pairs of open spiracles (one thoracic, one abdominal); the rest are closed

- More spiracles open progressively in subsequent instars to meet increasing oxygen demand

- Tracheal system grows and becomes more extensive with each moult

- During moulting, the cuticular lining of the tracheae is shed along with the exoskeleton

- In the pupal stage, the larval tracheal system undergoes extensive remodelling to give rise to the adult respiratory system

- Adult moths have all spiracles open and functional, with well-developed air sacs to support flight

The silkworm has a well-developed tracheal respiratory system that delivers oxygen directly to the cells and removes carbon dioxide. The system undergoes significant changes during development to meet the changing respiratory needs of the growing larva and metamorphosing pupa. Efficient gas exchange, especially in the silk glands, is crucial for the silkworm's main function of producing large amounts of silk. Understanding the structure and function of the silkworm respiratory system is important for optimizing rearing conditions and silk yield in sericulture.

Excretory System

Introduction to Excretory System of Silkworm

The excretory system of the silkworm, *Bombyx mori*, is responsible for the removal of metabolic wastes and the maintenance of homeostasis. It consists primarily of the Malpighian tubules, which are the main excretory organs, and associated structures like the hindgut and the rectum.

Structure of Malpighian Tubules and Their Function

Malpighian tubules are long, thin, blind-ended tubules that originate at the junction of the midgut and hindgut. In B. mori, there are six Malpighian tubules, arranged in three pairs. Each tubule is divided into three regions: proximal, middle, and distal.

1. Proximal region: This region is attached to the alimentary canal at the midgut-hindgut junction. It has a narrow lumen and is involved in the active transport of ions and water from the hemolymph into the tubule lumen.

2. Middle region: This is the longest part of the tubule and is the main site of uric acid secretion. The cells in this region have numerous microvilli and mitochondria, indicating their active role in transport processes.

3. Distal region: This is the blind end of the tubule, which is bathed in hemolymph. It is involved in the reabsorption of water and certain ions from the tubule lumen back into the hemolymph.

The main function of the Malpighian tubules is to filter the hemolymph and remove metabolic wastes, particularly nitrogenous compounds like uric acid. They also play a crucial role in maintaining the ionic and osmotic balance of the hemolymph.

Physiology of Excretion in Silkworm

The excretory process in B. mori involves several steps:

1. Ultrafiltration: Hemolymph enters the Malpighian tubules due to the osmotic gradient created by the active transport of ions (mainly potassium) into the tubule lumen. This draws water into the tubules by osmosis, carrying with it small molecules like metabolic wastes.

2. Secretion: The cells of the Malpighian tubules actively secrete uric acid and other waste products into the tubule lumen. This process requires energy in the form of ATP.

3. Reabsorption: As the filtrate moves along the tubule, the distal region reabsorbs water and certain ions (like potassium and chloride) back into the hemolymph. This concentrates the waste products in the tubule lumen.

4. Excretion: The concentrated waste products are then passed into the hindgut and rectum, where further water reabsorption occurs. The final excretory product, a semi-solid pellet containing uric acid crystals, is expelled through the anus.

The excretory system of B. mori is adapted to conserve water and ions while efficiently removing metabolic wastes. Uric acid is the main nitrogenous excretory product in terrestrial insects like silkworms, as it requires less water for its elimination compared to ammonia or urea.

In addition to the Malpighian tubules, other tissues like the fat body and the integument also play minor roles in excretion and osmoregulation in silkworms.

Understanding the structure and function of the excretory system is important for maintaining the health and productivity of silkworms in sericulture. Factors that disrupt excretory processes, such as diseases or environmental stressors, can negatively impact silkworm growth and silk production.

Nervous System

Anatomy of the Nervous System

The silkworm has a ventral nerve cord type of nervous system, which is typical of insects. The main components of the nervous system are:

1. Brain (Supraesophageal ganglion)

  - Consists of three fused ganglia: protocerebrum, deutocerebrum, and tritocerebrum

  - Located dorsally in the head capsule, above the oesophagus

  - Protocerebrum is the largest part and contains the central body and mushroom bodies, which are involved in sensory integration, learning, and memory

  - Deutocerebrum receives sensory input from the antennae and connects to the tritocerebrum

- Tritocerebrum innervates the labrum and integrates sensory information from the foregut

2. Subesophageal ganglion

- Lies ventrally in the head, below the oesophagus

- Formed by the fusion of mandibular, maxillary, and labial ganglia

- Innervates the mouthparts and the salivary glands

3. Ventral nerve cord

- Consists of a series of segmental ganglia connected by longitudinal connectives and transverse commissures

- Runs along the ventral midline of the thorax and abdomen

- Each thoracic segment has a ganglion that innervates the legs and wings

- Abdominal ganglia innervate the muscles and organs of the corresponding segments

- The last abdominal ganglion is larger and innervates the reproductive organs and the posterior gut

4. Stomatogastric nervous system

- Consists of frontal ganglion, hypocerebral ganglion, and ventricular ganglion

- Innervates the foregut, midgut, and hindgut

- Regulates the movements of the alimentary canal and enzyme secretion

5. Peripheral nervous system

- Includes sensory neurons, motor neurons, and neurosecretory cells

- Sensory neurons receive input from sensory receptors and relay information to the central nervous system

- Motor neurons innervate muscles and glands, controlling their activity

- Neurosecretory cells release hormones that regulate growth, development, and metabolism

Physiology of the Nervous System

1. Sensory processing

- The silkworm has various sensory receptors for detecting chemical, mechanical, visual, and thermal stimuli

- Chemoreceptors on the antennae, mouthparts, and tarsi detect olfactory and gustatory cues

- Mechanoreceptors, such as hair plates and chordotonal organs, respond to touch, vibration, and proprioception

- Compound eyes and stemmata (larval eyes) are involved in visual perception

- Thermoreceptors and hygroreceptors detect temperature and humidity changes

2. Motor control

- Motor neurons innervate skeletal muscles, controlling locomotion, feeding, and other behaviours

- The central pattern generators in the thoracic and abdominal ganglia coordinate rhythmic movements like crawling and spinning

- Neuromodulators, such as biogenic amines and neuropeptides, modulate the activity of motor circuits

3. Neuroendocrine regulation

- Neurosecretory cells in the brain and ventral nerve cord release hormones that regulate various physiological processes

- The prothoracicotropic hormone (PTTH) from the brain stimulates the prothoracic glands to produce ecdysone, triggering moulting and metamorphosis

- Insulin-like peptides from the brain regulate growth, metabolism, and reproduction

- Diapause hormone and pheromone biosynthesis activating neuropeptide (PBAN) control diapause and pheromone production, respectively

4. Neuronal plasticity and learning

- The mushroom bodies in the brain are involved in olfactory learning and memory formation

- Experience-dependent plasticity in the nervous system allows the silkworm to adapt to environmental changes and modify its behaviour

- Habituation, sensitization, and associative learning have been demonstrated in the silkworm

Development of the Nervous System

- The nervous system develops from the neuroectoderm during embryogenesis

- Neuroblasts, the neural stem cells, undergo asymmetric divisions to generate ganglion mother cells, which further divide to produce neurons and glial cells

- Axon guidance molecules, such as Robo and Slit, direct the growth and pathfinding of axons to establish the correct connectivity

- Programmed cell death (apoptosis) eliminates excess neurons and refines the neural circuits

- During metamorphosis, the nervous system undergoes extensive remodelling to adapt to the changes in body structure and behaviour

- Hormones, particularly ecdysone and juvenile hormone, regulate the development and plasticity of the nervous system

The silkworm nervous system is a relatively simple yet highly organized and adaptable structure that controls various aspects of the insect's life, from sensory perception and motor control to neuroendocrine regulation and learning. Understanding the anatomy, physiology, and development of the silkworm nervous system not only provides insights into the basic principles of neural function but also has implications for improving sericulture practices and developing novel strategies for pest control.

Reproductive system

Reproductive System in Larva

In the larval stage, the reproductive organs are not yet fully developed. However, the gonads (testes in males and ovaries in females) are present as rudimentary structures. These immature gonads grow and differentiate during the larval development, preparing for the adult stage.

Male Reproductive System

The male reproductive system of the silkworm moth consists of a pair of testes, vasa deferentia, seminal vesicles, accessory glands, ejaculatory duct, and external genitalia.

1. Testes

  - Paired, kidney-shaped organs located in the 5th abdominal segment

- Composed of four follicles, each containing numerous testicular tubules

- Spermatogenesis occurs in the testicular tubules, producing bundles of spermatozoa

2. Vasa Deferentia

- Paired ducts that arise from the testes and transport spermatozoa

- Dilated posteriorly to form the seminal vesicles

3. Seminal Vesicles

- Enlarged portions of the vasa deferentia that store and nourish spermatozoa

- Secrete nutrients and substances that promote sperm maturation and motility

4. Accessory Glands

- Paired, tubular glands that open into the vasa deferentia near the ejaculatory duct

- Secrete components of the seminal fluid that nourish and protect spermatozoa

5. Ejaculatory Duct

- Formed by the union of the vasa deferentia

- Muscular duct that expels spermatozoa during mating

6. External Genitalia

- Consists of the aedeagus (penis) and associated structures

- Used for transferring spermatozoa to the female during copulation

Female Reproductive System

The female reproductive system of the silkworm moth includes a pair of ovaries, lateral oviducts, common oviduct, spermatheca, accessory glands, and external genitalia.

1. Ovaries

- Paired, elongated organs located in the abdominal cavity

- Each ovary consists of four ovarioles that produce eggs (ova)

- Oogenesis occurs in the ovarioles, with eggs maturing in a linear sequence

2. Lateral Oviducts

- Paired ducts that arise from the ovaries and transport mature eggs

- Join posteriorly to form the common oviduct

3. Common Oviduct

- Formed by the union of the lateral oviducts

- Muscular duct that expels eggs during oviposition

4. Spermatheca

- A sac-like structure connected to the common oviduct

- Stores and nourishes spermatozoa received from the male during mating

- Releases spermatozoa for fertilizing the eggs as they pass through the common oviduct

5. Accessory Glands

- Paired glands that open into the common oviduct

- Secrete substances that form the egg chorion (shell) and adhesive for attaching eggs to the substrate

6. External Genitalia

- Consists of the ovipositor and associated structures

- Used for depositing fertilized eggs on a suitable substrate

Reproductive Physiology

- Mating occurs soon after the adult moths emerge from the cocoons

- Males locate females using sex pheromones and engage in a complex courtship behaviour

- During copulation, the male transfers a spermatophore containing spermatozoa into the female's bursa copulatrix

- Spermatozoa migrate from the bursa copulatrix to the spermatheca for storage

- As mature eggs pass through the common oviduct, they are fertilized by spermatozoa released from the spermatheca

- Fertilized eggs are deposited on a suitable substrate, such as mulberry leaves, where they will hatch into larvae

The reproductive system of the silkworm moth is adapted for efficient gamete production, mating, and oviposition. Understanding the structure and function of the reproductive organs is crucial for optimizing silkworm breeding and egg production in sericulture.

Silk Glands

Anatomy of the Silk Glands

The silk glands are a pair of long, tubular labial glands that lie ventral to the alimentary canal in the silkworm larva. In a fully grown 5th instar larva, the highly developed silk glands occupy a large portion of the body cavity. Each gland consists of three distinct regions:

Posterior Region

The posterior region (posterior division) is highly folded and tubular. It is attached to tracheal bushes that supply oxygen. This region synthesizes and secretes the main protein component of silk called fibroin, which makes up the core of the silk fibre. The fibroin is secreted into the lumen in a liquid state.

Middle Region

The middle region is the longest and widest part, folded into a W-shape with posterior, middle and anterior limbs. The cells lining the posterior limb secrete sericin-I, the middle limb secretes sericin-II, and the anterior limb secretes sericin-III. Sericins are glue-like proteins that coat and cement the fibroin, allowing the two fibroin filaments to stick together into a single fibre. The middle region also stores the liquid fibroin, allowing it to mature before spinning.

Anterior Region

The anterior region (anterior division) is thin and tubular. It does not have a secretory function but transports the silk solution to the spinneret for spinning the cocoon fiber. The cells here have a very thick inner lining called the cuticular intima that is shed during each larval molt.

Histology of the Silk Glands

Histologically, the silk gland wall is composed of three layers from outside to inside:

1) An outer tunica propria

2) A middle glandular epithelium that synthesizes the silk proteins

3) An inner cuticular intima lining the lumen

The silk gland cells are large and polyploid to support high rates of silk protein synthesis. Their nuclei become increasingly branched and convoluted in later larval stages, especially in the posterior and middle regions, to further enhance silk production.

Accessory Structures

Near the exit of the anterior region, the silk gland joins the duct of the Filippi's gland (Lyonet's gland), a pair of accessory glands thought to secrete a lubricating or waxy substance into the silk fibre as it is spun.

The anterior region terminates in a spinneret, a structure on the larval mouthpart that draws the liquid silk out and shapes it into a solid filament as it exits and contacts the air. Muscles surrounding the spinneret, called the silk press, help control the extrusion of silk.

The highly specialized silk glands take up proteins and nutrients from the silkworm's blood and convert them into large quantities of fibroin and sericin. These proteins are secreted into the gland lumen, transported to the spinneret, and spun out as a double strand of silk filament used by the larva to construct its cocoon. The silk glands are an essential organ enabling the silkworm to produce one of the most prized natural fibres.

Different silkworm strains and their characteristics

Strain	Origin	Voltinism	Cocoon Color	Cocoon Shape	Silk Quality	Other Traits
CSR2	India	Bivoltine	White	Oval	High	Tolerant to high temperature and humidity
CSR4	India	Bivoltine	White	Oval	High	High pupation rate and cocoon yield
CSR5	India	Bivoltine	White	Dumbbell	High	Shorter larval duration
NB4D2	India	Bivoltine	White	Oval	High	High cocoon weight and shell ratio
Pure Mysore	India	Multivoltine	Greenish yellow	Spindle	Low	Longer larval duration, good combiner with bivoltine breeds
Nistari	India	Multivoltine	Golden yellow	Spindle	Low	Hardy, tolerant to diseases and temperature fluctuations
Cambodge	Cambodia	Multivoltine	Yellow	Peanut	Medium	Produces fine, strong silk
Moria	Japan	Bivoltine	White	Peanut	High	High productivity and silk quality

Some key points about these strains:

- Bivoltine strains like CSR and NB4D2 from India, Moria and Ichinose from Japan, and Kinshu and Xinhui from China are known for high quality silk, productivity, and tolerance to environmental stresses.

- Multivoltine strains like Pure Mysore and Nistari from India are more hardy and disease resistant but produce lower quality silk. They are often used in crosses with bivoltine strains.

- Cambodge from Cambodia is a multivoltine strain known for its fine, strong silk.

- Cocoon colour, shape, and other economic traits vary between strains. For example, Pure Mysore has greenish-yellow spindle-shaped cocoons while CSR strains have white oval cocoons.

- Researchers evaluate silkworm strains based on traits like larval duration, cocoon weight, shell weight, silk ratio, filament length, and environmental adaptability to select parents for breeding programs.

A diverse set of silkworm strains with unique characteristics are maintained and utilized in different countries for silk production and genetic improvement of the silkworm.

Silkworm genetics and breeding

Silkworm genetics and breeding play a crucial role in improving silk production and quality. The domesticated silkworm, *Bombyx mori*, has been subjected to selective breeding for centuries, resulting in the development of various strains and hybrids with desirable traits. Understanding the genetic makeup of silkworms and employing appropriate breeding strategies are essential for enhancing sericulture productivity and sustainability.

Genetic Makeup and Inheritance

The silkworm, *Bombyx mori*, has a diploid chromosome number of 28 (n=28). The sex determination system in silkworms is unique, with females being heterogametic (ZW) and males being homogametic (ZZ). This contrasts with the more common XX/XY system found in many other organisms.

Silkworms exhibit a wide range of genetic variations, including morphological, physiological, and behavioural traits. These variations are influenced by both genetic and environmental factors. Some of the important traits that have been studied and manipulated through breeding include:

1. Voltinism: The number of life cycles completed by a silkworm in a year. Univoltine strains complete one life cycle per year, bivoltine strains complete two, and multivoltine strains complete multiple life cycles.

2. Cocoon characteristics: Traits such as cocoon weight, shell weight, shell ratio, filament length, and reelability are crucial for silk production and quality.

3. Disease resistance: Resistance to various diseases, such as grasserie (caused by a protozoan), flacherie (caused by

bacteria), and viral diseases, is essential for maintaining healthy silkworm populations.

4. Environmental tolerance: Traits like tolerance to high temperatures, humidity, and other environmental stresses are important for adapting silkworms to different rearing conditions.

Breeding Strategies

Several breeding strategies have been employed to improve silkworm strains and develop superior hybrids. These include:

1. Inbreeding and selection: Inbreeding is used to develop homozygous lines with desirable traits, which can then be used as parental lines for hybrid production.

2. Hybridization: Crossing genetically diverse parental lines can result in hybrid vigor or heterosis, leading to improved performance in traits like cocoon weight, larval growth, and disease resistance.

3. Backcrossing: Backcrossing is used to introgress specific desirable traits from one strain into another, while retaining the overall genetic background of the recurrent parent.

4. Mutation breeding: Induced mutations, either through physical or chemical mutagens, can generate novel genetic variations that can be exploited for breeding purposes.

5. Molecular breeding: With the advent of molecular techniques, marker-assisted selection (MAS) and genomic

selection are being employed to accelerate the breeding process and improve the accuracy of selection.

Hybrid Vigor and Hybrid Development

One of the most significant achievements in silkworm breeding has been the exploitation of hybrid vigor or heterosis. Hybrid silkworms, produced by crossing genetically diverse parental lines, often exhibit superior performance in terms of cocoon yield, larval growth, and disease resistance compared to their parents.

The development of hybrid silkworms involves several steps:

1. Identification and maintenance of genetically diverse parental lines.

2. Evaluation of parental lines and their combining ability.

3. Production of hybrid seeds through controlled crosses.

4. Performance evaluation of hybrid progenies under different environmental conditions.

5. Large-scale multiplication and distribution of superior hybrid seeds.

Various types of hybrids have been developed, including single-cross hybrids, double-cross hybrids, and three-way cross hybrids, each with its own advantages and applications.

Future Prospects

The integration of modern biotechnological tools, such as genomics, transcriptomics, and genome editing, holds great promise for advancing silkworm genetics and breeding. These technologies can facilitate the identification of genes and molecular markers associated with important traits, enabling more precise and efficient selection and breeding strategies.

Additionally, the development of transgenic silkworms and the application of genome editing techniques like CRISPR/Cas9 open up new avenues for introducing desirable traits or modifying existing ones, potentially leading to the creation of superior silkworm strains with enhanced productivity, disease resistance, and environmental adaptability.

Overall, silkworm genetics and breeding play a pivotal role in improving silk production and quality, ensuring the sustainability and profitability of the sericulture industry. Continuous research and innovation in this field are essential for meeting the growing demand for silk while addressing the challenges posed by changing environmental conditions and emerging diseases.

Chapter 4

Silkworm Rearing

Rearing house and equipment

Importance of Silkworm Rearing Houses

Silkworms are domesticated insects that require specific environmental conditions for optimal growth and cocoon production. A well-designed silkworm rearing house provides the ideal temperature, humidity, ventilation, lighting, and hygiene for the silkworms to thrive. The quality and yield of silk cocoons are directly impacted by the conditions inside the rearing house.

Location and Orientation

The location of the silkworm rearing house should be carefully selected. It should be built on an elevated, dry, sunny and well-ventilated site. In temperate and subtropical regions, the house should be constructed in a north-south direction, while in tropical regions, an east-west orientation is preferred with doors facing north and windows facing north-south. The house should be away from other buildings, noisy areas, and water-logged sites.

Size and Dimensions

The size of the rearing house depends on the quantity of silkworms being reared. A floor area of approximately 400 sq ft can accommodate rearing space for 100 disease-free layings (dfls), which is about 50,000 larvae. The building should be about 9-10 feet in height and each room should be more than 12-15 feet wide. A broad verandah of at least 6-8 feet wide should surround the building on all sides.

Construction Materials

The rearing house should be a permanent structure with brick walls and a roof made of asbestos sheets or reinforced cement concrete (RCC). The roof should be lined with materials like coconut fronds or straw in hot regions to maintain cooler temperatures inside. The floor should be cemented and rat-proof. Sufficient windows should be provided for proper ventilation and lighting.

Room Layout

The rearing house should have separate rooms for:

1. Chawki (young age) silkworm rearing

2. Late age silkworm rearing

3. Leaf storage and preservation

4. Mounting and spinning of mature larvae

5. Storage of rearing equipment and appliances

An anteroom serves as a changing area for workers to maintain hygiene.

Rearing Methods

Two main methods are used for rearing silkworms:

1. Shelf Rearing: Silkworms are reared on shelves or racks arranged in tiers up to 10 high. This vertical arrangement allows for rearing more silkworms in limited space.

2. Shoot Rearing: Whole mulberry shoots with leaves are provided to the worms on lower tiers. This method saves labour but requires more horizontal space.

Environmental Control

The rearing house should be designed to maintain a temperature of 24-28°C and relative humidity of 70-85%. Adequate ventilation is crucial to remove excess humidity and harmful gases. Lighting of around 15-30 lux is preferred by young silkworms. Cooling and humidifying systems may be needed in hot and dry weather, while heating may be required in colder conditions.

Hygiene and Disinfection

Maintaining hygiene is critical in sericulture. The rearing house and equipment should be thoroughly disinfected before each rearing cycle. Strict schedules are followed for cleaning, washing, and disinfection using materials like bleaching powder, slaked lime, and chlorine dioxide. Proper hygiene helps prevent disease outbreaks in silkworms.

A well-constructed and managed silkworm rearing house is essential for producing high-quality silk cocoons. Proper location, size, construction, layout, environmental control, and hygiene are key factors in the success of silkworm rearing.

Equipments

Rearing House

A well-designed rearing house is crucial for successful silkworm rearing. It should have adequate space, proper ventilation, and facilities to maintain optimal temperature and humidity. The rearing house typically includes:

- A main rearing hall for late-age silkworms

- Separate rooms for young silkworm (chawki) rearing, leaf storage, and rearing equipment storage

- Proper lighting and ventilation systems

- Facilities to maintain temperature between 24-28°C and relative humidity between 70-85%

Rearing Stands and Trays

Rearing stands, also known as racks or shelves, are used to hold the rearing trays in a vertical arrangement. They are typically made of wood, bamboo, or metal and have multiple tiers to maximize space utilization. The standard size is around 2.5m high, 1.5m long, and 0.65-1.0m wide, with 10-12 cross bars to accommodate the trays.

Rearing trays are portable containers used for keeping the silkworms during rearing. They are placed on the rearing stands and can be made of wood, bamboo, or plastic. Common sizes include:

- Rectangular wooden trays: 3.5' x 2.5'

- Circular bamboo trays: 3.5' to 4' diameter

- Plastic trays: 900mm L x 600mm W x 80mm H

Leaf Chopping and Storage Equipment

Mulberry leaves, the primary food for silkworms, need to be chopped into appropriate sizes based on the silkworm's age. Equipment used for this purpose includes:

- Leaf chopping board and knives

- Leaf chopping machine (for large-scale rearing)

- Leaf preservation chamber or room with temperature and humidity control

Environmental Control Equipment

Maintaining optimal temperature and humidity is crucial for silkworm health and growth. Equipment used for this purpose includes:

- Room heaters and humidifiers

- Air coolers and ventilation systems

- Wet and dry bulb thermometers or digital hygrometers to monitor temperature and humidity

Cleaning and Hygiene Equipment

Maintaining hygiene is essential to prevent disease outbreaks in silkworms. Equipment used for cleaning and disinfection includes:

- Power sprayers and dusters for applying disinfectants

- Bed cleaning nets to separate silkworms from litter

- Plastic crates and basins for handling silkworms and leaves

- Disinfectants like bleaching powder, slaked lime, and chlorine dioxide

Silkworm Handling Tools

Delicate handling of silkworms, especially in the young stages, is important to minimize injury and stress. Tools used for this purpose include:

- Feathers for brushing newly hatched larvae

- Plastic or bamboo chopsticks for picking and transferring larvae

- Forceps for removing dead or diseased larvae

Mountages for Cocoon Spinning

When mature silkworms are ready to spin cocoons, they need suitable structures called mountages. These can be:

- Rotary mountages made of plastic or bamboo

- Chandrika's or collapsible plastic mountages

- Bamboo or plastic spinning trays

Other essential equipment includes silkworm egg incubation frames, cocoon harvesting tools, and silk reeling machines for post-cocoon processing.

A wide range of equipment is used in silkworm rearing to ensure optimal growth, health, and cocoon production. Proper selection and maintenance of this equipment, along with good rearing practices, are key to successful sericulture.

Young age and late age rearing techniques

Young Age (Chawki) Rearing

Young age or chawki rearing refers to the rearing of silkworms from the time of hatching up to the second molt. This stage is crucial as the young worms are susceptible to diseases and environmental fluctuations.

Brushing

- Brushing is the process of separating newly hatched larvae from the egg sheets and transferring them to the rearing trays.

- It is done using a fine brush or feather when most of the eggs have hatched, usually around 9-10 AM.

Leaf Selection and Feeding

- Young silkworms require tender, succulent, and nutritious leaves.

- Leaves are selected from the top 3rd or 4th position of the shoot, which are glossy and rich in moisture and nutrients.

- Leaves are chopped into small pieces of 0.5-1 cm for easy consumption.

- Worms are fed 3-4 times a day at regular intervals.

Environmental Conditions

- Temperature: 26-28°C

- Humidity: 85-90%

- Proper ventilation and hygiene are maintained to prevent diseases.

Spacing

- As the worms grow, they require more space to prevent overcrowding.

- Bed area is gradually increased after each molt to accommodate the growing larvae.

Moulting Care

- During moulting, silkworms stop feeding and undergo physiological changes.

- Bed should be kept dry and undisturbed during this phase.

- Moulted worms are carefully shifted to fresh trays for further rearing.

Late Age Rearing

Late age rearing starts from the third instar and continues until the worms mature and are ready for spinning. Late age worms have a voracious appetite and grow rapidly.

Leaf Feeding

- Whole leaves or shoots are fed to the late age worms.

- Feeding frequency is reduced to 2-3 times a day.

- Leaf quality and quantity are crucial for the growth and development of silkworms.

Bed Cleaning

- Regular removal of leftover leaves and faecal matter is essential to maintain hygiene.

- Bed cleaning is done using nets or by sprinkling slaked lime to dry the bed.

Spacing

- Adequate spacing is provided to the growing worms to prevent overcrowding and ensure proper ventilation.

- Bed area is increased by 4-5 times after each moult.

Environmental Conditions

- Temperature: 24-26°C

- Humidity: 70-80%

- Proper ventilation and air circulation are maintained to remove excess humidity and heat.

Mounting

- When the worms are ready for spinning (5th instar), they are transferred to mountages or Chandrika's.

- Mountages provide a suitable surface for the worms to spin their cocoons.

- Worms are mounted when they stop feeding, become translucent, and start searching for a place to spin.

Harvesting

- Cocoons are harvested 5-7 days after mounting.

- They are sorted based on quality and marketed for further processing.

Young age rearing focuses on providing a conducive environment and nutritious leaves for the delicate chawki worms. Late age rearing involves managing the rapidly growing worms, ensuring proper feeding, spacing, and environmental conditions until they mature and spin cocoons. Proper rearing techniques at both stages are crucial for the success of silkworm rearing and the production of high-quality cocoons.

Environmental conditions required for optimal growth

Temperature

Temperature plays a crucial role in the growth and development of silkworms. The ideal temperature range for silkworm rearing is between 23°C to 28°C. However, the optimal temperature varies slightly depending on the stage of the silkworm:

- Young age worms (1st to 3rd instar): 26-28°C

- Late age worms (4th and 5th instar): 23-25°C

Fluctuations in temperature beyond the optimal range can negatively impact the growth, health, and productivity of silkworms. High temperatures can lead to increased metabolic activity, faster growth, and shorter larval duration, while low temperatures result in slower growth and prolonged larval duration.

Humidity

Relative humidity is another critical factor in silkworm rearing. The ideal humidity range is between 70-85%, with slight variations based on the silkworm's age:

- Young age worms: 85-90%

- Late age worms: 70-75%

High humidity can lead to increased risk of diseases, while low humidity can cause dehydration and poor growth. Maintaining the right balance of humidity is essential for the healthy development of silkworms.

Ventilation

Proper ventilation in the rearing room is crucial to maintain optimal environmental conditions and prevent the buildup of harmful gases like carbon dioxide, carbon monoxide, and ammonia. Poor ventilation can lead to high humidity, disease outbreaks, and stunted growth. Adequate air circulation helps maintain the desired temperature and humidity levels.

Lighting

Light intensity influences the distribution of silkworms in the rearing bed. Young silkworms prefer dim light (15-30 lux), while late age worms can tolerate brighter light. Proper lighting ensures even distribution of the worms and prevents crowding, which can lead to uneven growth and disease spread.

Rearing Room Design

The design of the silkworm rearing room plays a significant role in maintaining optimal environmental conditions. The room should be constructed to allow proper ventilation, temperature control, and humidity regulation. Some key aspects of rearing room design include:

- East-west orientation for better temperature control

- Adequate number of windows and ventilators for air circulation

- False ceiling or insulated roof to reduce heat gain

- Provision for heating and cooling systems as needed

- Hygienic flooring and drainage system for easy cleaning and disinfection

Monitoring and Control

Regular monitoring and control of environmental conditions are essential for successful silkworm rearing. Temperature and humidity should be checked frequently using thermometers and hygrometers. Adjustments can be made using heating, cooling, humidification, or dehumidification systems as required. Automated environmental control systems can help maintain optimal conditions with minimal manual intervention.

Maintaining the ideal temperature, humidity, ventilation, lighting, and rearing room design is crucial for the optimal growth and development of silkworms. Careful monitoring and control of these environmental factors can help ensure high productivity and quality of cocoons in sericulture.

Feeding and care of silkworms

Feeding Mulberry Leaves

Silkworms feed exclusively on mulberry leaves. The quality and quantity of leaves directly impact the health and growth of the silkworms.

Leaf Selection

- Young silkworms (1st to 3rd instar) require tender, glossy, succulent leaves from the top of the mulberry plant.

- Mature silkworms (4th and 5th instar) can be fed mature leaves or whole shoots.

- Avoid feeding yellowed, diseased, or pest-infested leaves.

Leaf Harvesting and Storage

- Harvest leaves in the morning after the dew has evaporated.

- Store harvested leaves in a cool, ventilated place away from direct sunlight.

- Use the leaves within 24 hours of harvesting for optimal freshness and nutrition.

Chopping and Quantity

- Chop the leaves into small pieces for young silkworms to facilitate easy consumption.

- Gradually increase the size of leaf pieces as the silkworms grow.

- Feed young silkworms 3-4 times a day, while mature silkworms can be fed 2-3 times a day.

- Provide enough leaves to form a single layer on the rearing bed, avoiding overfeeding and underfeeding.

Feeding Silkworm Chow

Silkworm chow is an artificial diet that can be used as an alternative to mulberry leaves. It is convenient for year-round rearing.

- Mix the chow powder with water to form a paste and spread it on the rearing bed.

- Silkworms conditioned to chow may not readily accept mulberry leaves later, so maintain consistency in the diet.

- Follow the manufacturer's instructions for preparing and storing the chow.

Environmental Conditions

Maintaining optimal environmental conditions is crucial for silkworm health and growth.

Temperature

- Young silkworms: 26-28°C

- Mature silkworms: 24-26°C

- Avoid exposing silkworms to extreme temperatures or sudden fluctuations.

Humidity

- Young silkworms: 85-90% relative humidity

- Mature silkworms: 70-80% relative humidity

- Maintain humidity by hanging wet cloths or using humidifiers in the rearing room.

Ventilation and Lighting

- Ensure proper ventilation to remove excess humidity and harmful gases.

- Provide adequate lighting (15-30 lux) for even distribution of silkworms on the rearing bed.

Hygiene and Disease Prevention

Maintaining hygiene is essential to prevent disease outbreaks in silkworms.

Bed Cleaning

- Remove leftover leaves, faecal matter, and dead worms daily.

- Clean the rearing bed thoroughly after each moult and disinfect it before the next rearing cycle.

Handling and Quarantine

- Wash hands before handling silkworms or their food.

- Use separate tools for handling healthy and diseased silkworms.

- Isolate any diseased or abnormal silkworms in a separate container to prevent the spread of infection.

Disinfection

- Regularly disinfect the rearing room, equipment, and tools using approved disinfectants like bleach, lime, or formalin.

- Follow proper concentrations and exposure times to ensure effective disinfection without harming the silkworms.

Moulting and Mounting Care

Silkworms undergo four moults during their larval stage and require special care during these periods.

Moulting Care

- Recognize signs of impending moult, such as swollen head and immobility.

- Keep the rearing bed dry and undisturbed during moulting.

- Resume feeding only after all the worms have completed moulting.

Mounting

- Identify mature silkworms ready for spinning by their translucent, yellowish appearance and restless behaviour.

- Transfer mature silkworms to spinning trays or mountages with adequate space and ventilation.

- Ensure proper temperature and humidity during the spinning phase.

Proper feeding, environmental control, hygiene, and care during critical stages are essential for successful silkworm rearing. Attention to these factors helps ensure healthy growth, disease prevention, and high-quality cocoon production.

Chapter 5

Silkworm Diseases and Pests

Major silkworm diseases, their causes and prevention

Viral Diseases

1. Nuclear Polyhedrosis (Grasserie Disease)

Nuclear polyhedrosis, also known as grasserie disease, is one of the most serious viral diseases in silkworms. It is caused by the *Bombyx mori* nucleopolyhedrovirus (BmNPV).

Causes

- High temperature and humidity

- Feeding silkworms contaminated mulberry leaves containing viral polyhedra

- Poor hygiene and rearing conditions

Symptoms

- Loss of appetite and sluggish movement

- Swollen, shiny skin with inter-segmental bulges

- Release of milky white or yellowish fluid containing polyhedral bodies

- Translucent anterior part of the body

- Larvae eventually die and turn black, rupturing easily

Prevention

- Maintain proper hygiene and disinfection of rearing rooms and equipment

- Avoid feeding silkworms yellowed, diseased, or pest-infested mulberry leaves

- Isolate and dispose of infected larvae immediately

- Use disease-resistant silkworm breeds

- Control temperature and humidity in the rearing environment

2. Cytoplasmic Polyhedrosis

Cytoplasmic polyhedrosis is caused by the *Bombyx mori* cytoplasmic polyhedrosis virus (BmCPV). It specifically infects the silkworm midgut where viral multiplication occurs.

Causes

- Ingestion of contaminated mulberry leaves containing BmCPV polyhedra

- Poor hygiene and rearing conditions

Symptoms

- Sluggishness and loss of appetite

- Swollen, translucent, and fragile appearance

- Emission of soft feces

- White wrinkles in the posterior midgut

Prevention

- Maintain proper hygiene and disinfection of rearing rooms and equipment

- Avoid feeding silkworms contaminated mulberry leaves

- Isolate and dispose of infected larvae

- Control temperature and humidity in the rearing environment

3. Infectious Flacherie

Infectious flacherie is caused by infectious flacherie virus (IFV) often in combination with bacterial infections. The virus enters the silkworm body orally with contaminated mulberry leaves.

Causes

- Ingestion of leaves contaminated with IFV

- Secondary bacterial infections

- Poor hygiene and rearing conditions

Symptoms

- Loss of appetite and vomiting

- Diarrhea and emission of soft feces

- Flaccid and fragile body

- Foul odor from diseased larvae

Prevention

- Feed silkworms with healthy, hygienic mulberry leaves

- Maintain proper hygiene and disinfection of rearing rooms and equipment

- Isolate and dispose of infected larvae

- Control temperature and humidity in the rearing environment

The major viral diseases of silkworm - nuclear polyhedrosis, cytoplasmic polyhedrosis, and infectious flacherie - are caused by BmNPV, BmCPV, and IFV respectively. They are transmitted orally through contaminated mulberry leaves and facilitated by poor rearing conditions.

Prevention relies on maintaining strict hygiene, proper disinfection, optimal environmental control, and prompt isolation of infected larvae. Using disease-resistant silkworm breeds and avoiding already infected mulberry leaves are also important preventive measures against these economically damaging viral diseases in sericulture.

Bacterial Diseases

1. Flacherie (Mukhlaga)

Flacherie, also known as Mukhlaga, is one of the most common bacterial diseases in silkworms. It is mainly caused by the infection of Bacillus, **Streptococcus**, and **Staphylococcus** bacteria, often in combination with viral infections.

Causes

- Ingestion of contaminated mulberry leaves containing pathogenic bacteria

- Poor hygiene and rearing conditions, such as improper bed cleaning, feeding wet leaves, and accumulation of feces

- Fluctuating temperature and humidity

- Overcrowding of silkworms

Symptoms

- Loss of appetite and sluggish movement

- Softening and flaccidity of the body

- Emission of foul odor

- Diarrhea and vomiting

- Silkworms become thin and inactive

Prevention

- Maintain proper hygiene and disinfection of rearing rooms and equipment

- Avoid feeding silkworms contaminated or wet mulberry leaves

- Isolate and dispose of infected larvae immediately

- Maintain optimal temperature and humidity conditions

- Avoid overcrowding of silkworms

- Regular bed cleaning to remove feces and litter

2.Bacterial Septicemia

Bacterial septicemia is another serious bacterial disease that affects silkworms. It is caused by the infection of **Streptococcus** and **Staphylococcus** bacteria, often secondary to viral infections.

Causes

- Poor rearing conditions and hygiene

- Secondary infection to viral diseases

- Injury or wounds on silkworm body

Symptoms

- Sluggish movement and loss of appetite

- Softening and flaccidity of the body

- Emission of foul odor

- Swollen body with shrunken posterior part

- Oozing of black, foul-smelling liquid from cracked skin

Prevention

- Maintain proper hygiene and disinfection of rearing rooms and equipment

- Isolate and dispose of infected larvae immediately

- Handle silkworms carefully to avoid causing injury

- Control temperature and humidity in the rearing environment

- Disinfect rearing rooms and appliances with 2% formalin after rearing

3. Sotto Disease

Sotto disease is a toxicosis caused by the bacteria Bacillus sotto. The silkworms are affected by ingesting the bacterial toxin present on mulberry leaves.

Causes

- Ingestion of mulberry leaves contaminated with ***Bacillus sotto*** toxin

- Presence of Bacillus sotto in diseased larvae, mulberry leaves, air, and water

Symptoms

- Sudden diarrhoea in 4th and 5th instar larvae

- Vomiting of fluid

- Softening, putrefaction, and shrinkage of the body

- Black or red coloration of the body

Prevention

- Prevent silkworms from ingesting the toxic substance by maintaining hygiene

- Isolate and destroy infected silkworms

- Disinfect rearing rooms and equipment

- Maintain optimal rearing conditions to raise healthy and strong silkworms

The major bacterial diseases of silkworm - flacherie, bacterial septicemia, and sotto disease - are caused by various pathogenic bacteria, often in combination with other factors like viral infections, poor hygiene, and improper rearing conditions.

Prevention relies on maintaining strict hygiene, proper disinfection, optimal environmental control, and prompt isolation of infected larvae. Feeding silkworms with healthy, uncontaminated mulberry leaves and avoiding overcrowding are also crucial in preventing these economically damaging bacterial diseases in sericulture.

Fungal Diseases

1. White Muscardine

White muscardine is one of the most common and virulent fungal diseases in silkworms. It poses a major threat to silk cocoon production, especially during rainy and winter seasons.

Causal Organism

White muscardine is caused by the entomopathogenic fungus ***Beauveria bassiana***. The fungus produces white powdery asexual spores (conidia) on the cuticle of infected silkworm cadavers. These conidia serve as the infective propagules.

Symptoms

- Loss of appetite and inactivity in infected larvae

- Presence of moist specks on the skin

- Vomiting and flaccidity of the body

- After death, the larva hardens, followed by mummification due to growth of white aerial mycelia and conidia over the body

Mode of Transmission

- Ingestion of mulberry leaves contaminated with *B. bassiana* spores

- Direct contact with infected silkworms or contaminated rearing surfaces

- High humidity and low temperature favor the growth and spread of the fungus

Prevention and Control

- Maintain proper hygiene and disinfection of rearing rooms and equipment

- Avoid high humidity (above 90%) and low temperature (below 25°C) in the rearing environment

- Isolate and dispose of infected larvae immediately

- Apply bed disinfectants like Vijetha supplement, Resham Jyothi, or Dithane M45

- Dust slaked lime or formalin-soaked chaff in rearing trays to prevent fungal growth

- Use of fungicides like Labex (a mixture of lime and bleaching powder) can control muscardine

2. Green Muscardine

Green muscardine is another serious fungal disease of silkworms, particularly prevalent during hot and humid conditions.

Causal Organism

Green muscardine is caused by the entomopathogenic fungus *Metarhizium anisopliae* (formerly *Nomuraea rileyi*). The fungus produces bright green asexual spores (conidia) on the surface of infected silkworm cadavers.

Symptoms

- Sluggishness and oil-colored specks on the larval body

- Cadavers become soft at first, then stiffen and get covered with bright green conidia

- Hemolymph appears turbid and gradually fills with beaded hyphal bodies or hyphae

Mode of Transmission

- Ingestion of mulberry leaves contaminated with M. anisopliae spores

- Direct contact with infected silkworms or contaminated rearing surfaces

- Hot and humid conditions favor the growth and spread of the fungus

Prevention and Control

- Maintain proper ventilation and avoid high humidity in the rearing room

- Isolate and dispose of infected larvae immediately

- Disinfect the rearing room, equipment, and surroundings with recommended fungicides

- Apply bed disinfectants to prevent fungal growth

- Avoid injury to silkworms during handling to prevent fungal entry through wounds

3. Aspergillosis (Brown Muscardine)

Aspergillosis, also known as brown muscardine, is a fungal disease that commonly affects young silkworms. It is caused by several species of Aspergillus fungi.

Causal Organisms

Over 10 Aspergillus species are known to infect silkworms, with *A. flavus* and *A. tamarii* being the most common pathogens. The fungi produce brownish or greenish-yellow conidial layers on infected silkworms.

Symptoms

- Infected young larvae appear lustrous and die

- Dark green (*A. flavus*) or rusty brown (*A. tamarii*) mycelial clusters are seen on the dead body

Mode of Transmission

- Ingestion of mulberry leaves contaminated with Aspergillus spores

- Direct contact with infected silkworms or contaminated rearing surfaces

- High temperature and humidity favor the growth of Aspergillus fungi

Prevention and Control

- Maintain proper hygiene and avoid unhygienic rearing conditions

- Disinfect the rearing room and equipment with 2% formalin

- Apply bed disinfectants like Dithane M45 and kaolin after each moulting

- Avoid feeding silkworms with inferior quality or contaminated mulberry leaves

- Maintain optimal temperature and humidity in the rearing environment

White muscardine (***B. bassiana***), green muscardine (***M. anisopliae***), and aspergillosis (***Aspergillus spp.***) are the major fungal diseases affecting silkworms. These diseases can cause significant crop losses in sericulture. Maintaining proper hygiene, optimal environmental conditions, and timely application of disinfectants and fungicides are crucial for preventing and controlling these fungal diseases in silkworm rearing.

Protozoan Diseases

1. Pebrine (Phutuka)

Pebrine, also known as "Phutuka rog" or "pepper disease," is the most serious protozoan disease affecting silkworms, particularly the muga silkworm. It poses a significant threat to sericulture, causing heavy crop losses and even total crop failure in severe cases.

Causal Organism

Pebrine is caused by the protozoan parasite *Nosema bombycis*, belonging to the family Nosematidae. In India, the most virulent strains of this pathogen are NIK-2r, NIK-3h, and NIK-4m. The protozoan completes its life cycle through two stages: the infective spore stage and the vegetative stage.

Modes of Transmission

The disease is transmitted to silkworms through three different routes:

1. Transovarial (vertical) transmission: Infected mother moths pass the Nosema spores to their eggs, resulting in the hatching of infected larvae. This is the primary mode of transmission and the most difficult to control.

2. Oral (horizontal) transmission: Silkworm larvae can acquire the infection by ingesting mulberry leaves contaminated with Nosema spores from the feces of infected worms or dead larvae.

3. Contact transmission: Larvae can also get infected through their skin when they come in contact with Nosema

spores present in the rearing bed, contaminated by fecal matter or dead tissues.

Symptoms

The symptoms of pebrine vary depending on the stage of the silkworm's life cycle:

- **Egg:** Infected eggs may fail to hatch and appear pale yellow in color. They also show poor attachment to the egg card due to improper glue deposition.

- **Larvae:** Primary infected larvae usually die before exhibiting prominent symptoms. Secondary and tertiary infected larvae show loss of appetite, stunted and irregular growth (unequal size), incomplete molting (clean worm symptom), black pepper-like spots on the body, irregular brown patches, and soft feces. Infected larvae often die after spinning without pupating.

- **Pupa**: Live infected pupae inside the cocoon may have a black, swollen body with black spots on the sides of the abdomen.

- **Adult moth:** Infected moths exhibit black spots on the abdomen, deformed antennae, unstretched and discoloured wings. Females lay eggs in irregular, loose heaps, and body scales fall off easily.

Detection

Pebrine can be detected at any stage of the silkworm's life cycle by observing the above-mentioned symptoms. Microscopic examination of homogenates, body fluids, and fecal pellets can reveal the presence of Nosema spores.

Advanced immuno-enzymatic methods can also quickly detect the presence of pebrine spores.

Prevention and Control Measures

1. Use of disease-free silkworm eggs: Only certified disease-free eggs should be used for rearing. Microscopic examination of mother moths is crucial to eliminate infected eggs.

2. Isolation and disposal of infected larvae: Diseased larvae detected in the rearing bed should be immediately removed and incinerated to prevent the spread of infection.

3. Disinfection of rearing equipment and rooms: All rearing appliances, including the rearing room, should be thoroughly disinfected with 2-5% formalin or bleaching powder. Benomyl, Bavistin, or Bengard can be used as alternatives for disinfecting rearing accessories.

4. Egg surface disinfection: After microscopic examination, disease-free eggs should be treated with 2% formalin for 5 minutes to kill any surface contamination of pebrine spores.

5. Rearing of disease-resistant silkworm races: The use of disease-resistant silkworm races, such as Nistari, can help minimize the impact of pebrine.

Pebrine is a highly virulent protozoan disease that poses a significant threat to sericulture. Effective management of this disease relies on early detection, strict hygiene measures, disinfection of rearing equipment and rooms, and the use of disease-free eggs and resistant silkworm races. Implementing these preventive measures is crucial for minimizing crop losses and ensuring the sustainability of the sericulture industry.

Pests affecting silkworms and their management

1.Uzi Fly (*Exorista bombycis*)

The uzi fly is one of the most serious pests of the mulberry silkworm, *Bombyx mori*. It is an **endoparasitoid** that lays eggs on the silkworm larvae.

Life Cycle and Damage

- Female uzi flies lay 1-2 cream-colored eggs on each silkworm larva, preferring 4th or 5th instar larvae.

- Eggs hatch in 48-62 hours, and the maggots enter the silkworm's body, leaving a black scar at the entry point.

- Maggots feed inside the silkworm for 5-7 days, causing weakness and death. Affected larvae have a flaccid body and cannot spin cocoons.

- Mature maggots emerge from the dead silkworm, pupate, and develop into adult flies in 10-12 days.

Management

a. Exclusion Method:

   - Install wire mesh or nylon nets on windows and doors of the rearing house to prevent fly entry.

   - Use double-door system or anteroom at the entrance.

b. Uzi Traps:

- Place uzicide solution in white trays inside and outside the rearing house to attract and kill adult flies.

- Use yellow sticky traps or cards to trap flies.

c. Biological Control:

- Release *Nesolynx thymus*, an ecto-pupal parasitoid of the uzi fly, inside the rearing house.

- Use uzi parasitoid bags containing N. thymus near the rearing trays, mountages, and in the grainage.

d. Chemical Control:

- Apply uzicide solution (Dichlorvos) on the silkworm body during larval stages as per recommendation.

- Use uzi repellent and ovicidal dusts like Uzipowder, Uzicide, or Resham Keet Oushadh.

e. Cultural Practices:

- Collect and destroy uzi-infested silkworms and pupae.

- Maintain proper hygiene in the rearing room and surroundings.

- Dispose of silkworm litter and flimsy cocoons properly to prevent fly breeding.

2. Dermestid Beetles (*Dermestes spp.*)

Dermestid beetles are major pests of stored silkworm cocoons and pupae in grainages. They belong to the family Dermestidae and cause significant damage to silk cocoons.

Damage

- Adult beetles and larvae bore into the cocoons and eat the pupae, rendering the cocoons unfit for reeling.

- They also attack pierced cocoons, defective cocoons, and ovipositing silkmoths.

Management

Sanitation:

- Maintain cleanliness in the grainage and cocoon storage rooms.

- Avoid long-term storage of rejected cocoons and perished eggs.

- Disinfect the rooms regularly using 0.2% Malathion or other insecticides.

Physical Methods:

- Expose infested cocoons to sunlight for 2-3 hours to kill the grubs and adults.

- Use wire mesh screens on doors and windows to prevent beetle entry.

Chemical Methods:

- Store cocoons in Deltamethrin-treated bags.

- Fumigate the cocoons with ethylene dichloride and carbon tetrachloride mixture.

- Use naphthalene balls or camphor as repellents in the storage area.

3. Ants

Various species of ants, such as fire ants (***Solenopsis spp.***) and crazy ants (***Paratrechina longicornis***), can infest silkworm rearing houses and cause damage to the larvae and cocoons.

Damage

- Ants prey upon silkworm larvae and pupae, causing direct mortality.

- They cut the cocoons and damage the pupae inside, affecting silk quality.

Management

Sanitation:

- Keep the rearing room and surroundings clean and free from ant colonies.

- Dispose of silkworm litter and debris promptly.

Physical Barriers:

- Use water or sticky barriers around the rearing stands to prevent ant access.

- Seal cracks and crevices in the rearing room to eliminate ant entry points.

Chemical Control:

- Apply insecticidal baits or sprays in the affected areas, taking care not to contaminate the silkworms or their food.

- Use safer insecticides like boric acid, diatomaceous earth, or neem-based products.

Biological Control:

- Encourage natural enemies of ants, such as predatory insects or entomopathogenic fungi.

The uzi fly, dermestid beetles, and ants are major pests that can cause significant damage to silkworms and cocoons. Effective management involves a combination of exclusion, sanitation, physical barriers, biological control, and judicious use of insecticides. Implementing an integrated pest management (IPM) approach that focuses on prevention, monitoring, and eco-friendly control measures is crucial for sustainable pest management in sericulture.

Chapter 6

Silk Reeling and Processing

Harvesting and sorting of cocoons

Harvesting of Cocoons

The silkworm larvae spin their cocoons over a period of 3-8 days by moving their heads in a figure 8 motion, producing a silk filament composed primarily of fibroin protein.

Once the cocoons are fully formed, typically around 7-8 days after the larvae began spinning, they are carefully harvested by hand. This timing is crucial - if harvested too early, the silk filament will be incomplete, but if too late, the moth will have emerged, breaking the continuous filament.

Some cocoons may be cut open to inspect the pupae inside and check if they have fully developed before harvesting the rest. Fully formed pupae will appear plump and brown in color.

Stifling/Killing the Pupae of Silk

Stifling or killing the pupae inside the silk cocoons is a crucial step in the silk production process. It is done to prevent the emergence of the adult silk moth, which would otherwise break the continuous silk filament while coming out of the cocoon, rendering it unusable for reeling.

Purpose of Stifling

The primary purpose of stifling is to preserve the integrity of the silk cocoon and maintain the continuity of the silk filament. If the pupae are allowed to emerge as adult moths, they secrete an enzyme that dissolves the silk fibers, enabling them to break free from the cocoon. This process would result in the silk filament being cut into shorter lengths, making it unsuitable for reeling and producing high-quality silk thread.

Methods of Stifling

There are several methods employed for stifling or killing the pupae inside the cocoons. The choice of method depends on factors such as the scale of production, availability of resources, and local traditions.

1. Sun Drying

One of the oldest and most traditional methods of stifling is sun drying. In this method, the cocoons are spread out in the sun for several days, exposing them to direct sunlight and heat. The heat from the sun kills the pupae inside the cocoons and dries them out, making them suitable for storage and further processing.

2. Steam Stifling

Steam stifling is a widely used method in modern silk production facilities. In this process, the cocoons are placed in a perforated container or basket and exposed to hot steam for a specific duration, typically 10-20 minutes. The high temperature of the steam effectively kills the pupae inside the cocoons.

3. Hot Air Stifling

Similar to steam stifling, hot air stifling involves exposing the cocoons to hot air in a controlled environment. The cocoons are placed in a chamber or oven, and hot air is circulated around them at temperatures ranging from 60°C to 85°C for several hours. This method ensures that the pupae are killed while also drying the cocoons for better preservation.

Importance of Proper Stifling

Proper stifling is crucial for obtaining high-quality silk filaments and ensuring the longevity of the cocoons during storage. Inadequate stifling can lead to the emergence of adult moths, which can damage the silk filaments and render the cocoons unusable. Additionally, improper stifling can result in the growth of mold or other microorganisms, further degrading the quality of the silk.

After the stifling process, the cocoons are sorted, graded, and prepared for the next step in the silk production process, which is reeling or unwinding the continuous silk filament from the cocoons.

Sorting and Grading

Importance of Cocoon Sorting

Cocoon sorting is a crucial step in the silk production process. It involves separating the cocoons based on their quality and suitability for reeling. Proper sorting ensures that only the best cocoons are used for silk production, resulting in higher yields and better-quality silk. Unsorted or improperly sorted cocoons can lead to issues during reeling, such as frequent breakages, uneven silk quality, and lower productivity.

Criteria for Sorting

Cocoons are sorted based on various criteria, including:

1. **Size and Shape**

Cocoons of uniform size and shape are preferred for reeling. Larger cocoons generally yield more silk, while smaller or misshapen cocoons may be more prone to breakage during reeling. Cocoons that are too small or irregularly shaped are typically separated and used for other purposes, such as silk waste or spun silk.

2. **Weight and Compactness**

Heavier and more compact cocoons are desirable as they tend to have a higher silk content. Lighter or loosely spun cocoons may have a lower silk yield or be more susceptible to damage during reeling.

3. **Shell Ratio**

The shell ratio is the proportion of the cocoon shell weight to the total cocoon weight. Cocoons with a higher shell ratio (typically between 18-24%) are preferred as they contain more silk filament.

4. Surface Defects

Cocoons with surface defects, such as stains, holes, or deformities, are separated from the good cocoons. These defects can affect the reeling process and the quality of the silk produced.

Double or Multiple Cocoons

Double or multiple cocoons, where two or more silkworms have spun their cocoons together, are separated from the single cocoons. These cocoons are more challenging to reel and can lead to frequent breakages or tangling of the silk filaments.

Sorting Methods

Cocoon sorting can be performed manually or using automated machinery, depending on the scale of production and available resources.

1. Manual Sorting

In manual sorting, trained workers visually inspect and sort the cocoons based on the criteria mentioned above. This method is labor-intensive and time-consuming but can be effective for small-scale operations or when sorting for specific quality requirements.

2. Automated Sorting

Automated sorting machines use various techniques, such as image processing, weight measurement, and optical sensors, to sort cocoons based on predetermined parameters. These machines can process large volumes of cocoons quickly and consistently, reducing labor requirements and increasing efficiency.

Silk Reeling

Silk reeling is the process of extracting the continuous silk filament from the stifled cocoons. It is a delicate and skilled process that requires careful handling of the cocoons.

Cocoon Cooking

Before reeling, the cocoons are cooked or boiled in hot water at temperatures around 95-97°C for 10-15 minutes. This process softens the sericin (a gum-like protein) that binds the silk filaments together, making it easier to unwind the filaments without breaking.

Brushing and Deflossing

After cooking, the cocoons are brushed or deflossed to remove the outer loose fibers (floss) and find the end of the continuous silk filament. This is typically done by hand or using mechanical brushes.

Reeling

The reeling process involves unwinding the silk filaments from the cocoons and combining them into a single, continuous thread. Several methods are used for reeling, including:

Charka (Spinning Wheel)

This is a traditional method where the silk filaments from multiple cocoons are manually combined and reeled onto a spinning wheel. It produces silk of lower quality but is still widely used in cottage industries.

Cottage Basin

In this method, the cocoons are placed in a basin of hot water, and the silk filaments are manually combined and reeled onto a reel. It produces better quality silk than the charka method but is still labour-intensive.

Multiend Reeling

This is a modern, automated method where the silk filaments from multiple cocoons are combined and reeled onto a reel using machines. It produces high-quality silk with uniform thickness and minimal defects.

Re-reeling and Finishing

After the initial reeling, the silk thread is often re-reeled onto larger spools or skeins. This process helps to remove any remaining defects and produce a uniform, high-quality silk thread. The silk may also undergo additional finishing processes like degumming (removing the remaining sericin), bleaching, and dyeing before it is ready for weaving or other applications.

The reeling and processing of silk require skilled labor and careful handling to ensure the production of high-quality silk threads. Different techniques are employed depending on the scale of production and the desired quality of the silk.

Raw silk production and grading

Raw Silk Production

Raw silk is produced through a process called sericulture, which involves rearing silkworms to obtain silk cocoons. The key steps in raw silk production are:

1. Mulberry Cultivation

Silkworms primarily feed on mulberry leaves. Mulberry trees are cultivated to provide a steady supply of leaves for the silkworms. In India, most mulberry cultivation is done by small farmers.

2. Silkworm Rearing

Silkworm larvae, obtained from disease-free eggs, are reared in controlled environments with optimal temperature and humidity. They are fed chopped mulberry leaves in special trays. After 25-30 days of voracious feeding, the larvae start spinning their cocoons.

3. Cocoon Harvesting

Once the silkworms have completed spinning their cocoons, they are harvested. This usually happens 7-8 days after the start of spinning. The cocoons are carefully picked by hand to avoid damaging the delicate silk fibers.

4. Stifling and Sorting

To prevent the silkworm pupae from emerging and breaking the cocoons, they are killed by exposure to heat (stifling), using steam or hot air. Stifling also dries the cocoons for better preservation. The cocoons are then sorted based on quality parameters like size, shape, color and luster.

5. Reeling

Reeling is the process of unwinding the silk filaments from the cocoons to obtain raw silk threads. The cocoons are first boiled in water to soften the sericin gum holding the fibers together. Then, the filaments from several cocoons (usually 8-10) are reeled together to form a single thread. Reeling can be done by hand using a charkha or by semi-automatic or automatic machines.

6. Re-reeling and Twisting

The raw silk threads obtained by reeling are re-reeled to remove any remaining sericin and to even out the thickness. The threads are then twisted together to make the final silk yarn suitable for weaving or knitting.

Raw Silk Grading

The quality of raw silk is assessed and graded based on various parameters. China, the world's largest silk producer, has a national standard for grading raw silk (GB/T 1797-2008). It categorizes raw silk into 11 grades: 6A, 5A, 4A, 3A, 2A, A, B, C, D, E, and F, with 6A being the highest quality.

The main criteria used for grading raw silk are:

1. Fineness and size variation: The thickness of the silk filament and its uniformity along the length. Finer and more even threads are higher grade.

2. Cleanness: The amount of defects like loops, snarls, waste, etc. present. Cleaner silk with fewer defects gets a better grade.

3. Neatness: The level of entanglement or gumming up of the threads. Neater threads with less entanglement are graded higher.

4. Tenacity: The strength and elasticity of the silk filament. Stronger, more elastic threads indicate better quality.

5. Elongation: The degree to which the silk can stretch before breaking. A higher elongation at break is desirable.

6. Cohesion: How well the filaments stick together. Better cohesion means less breakage during processing.

In India, the Bureau of Indian Standards has laid out quality standards and testing methods for raw silk in IS 15090 (1-11). It specifies methods to test the above parameters and grade the silk accordingly.

High grade raw silk like the 5A and 6A varieties are used by luxury brands and fashion houses. Lower grades are more commonly used. Grading helps ensure quality standardization and fetches better prices for the silk producers.

Raw silk production is a multi-step process starting from silkworm rearing to obtaining the final silk yarn. Grading of the raw silk based on quality parameters is essential for maintaining standards and determining the end use and value of the silk. Producing high quality raw silk requires a combination of skilled sericulture practices and advanced reeling and testing technologies.

Byproducts of sericulture and their utilization

Sericulture, the cultivation of silkworms for silk production, generates a significant amount of byproducts and waste materials. These byproducts can be effectively utilized in various sectors, contributing to sustainable practices and generating additional revenue streams for the industry. The following sections discuss the different byproducts of sericulture and their potential applications.

Mulberry Waste

Mulberry leaves serve as the primary food source for silkworms. During mulberry cultivation and silkworm rearing, a substantial amount of leaf litter, pruned branches, and other plant waste accumulates. These waste materials can be effectively utilized in the following ways:

Vermicomposting: Mulberry waste can be converted into nutrient-rich vermicompost through the action of earthworms. The resulting compost can be used as an organic fertilizer for agricultural and horticultural applications, promoting sustainable farming practices.

Mushroom Cultivation: Mulberry waste, particularly the leaf litter and pruned branches, can serve as a substrate for cultivating edible and medicinal mushrooms, such as oyster mushrooms (Pleurotus spp.). This practice not only utilizes the waste but also contributes to food security and generates additional income.

Animal Feed: Dried mulberry leaves and branches can be used as a nutritious feed supplement for livestock, particularly ruminants like cattle and goats.

Mulberry Juice and Extracts: Mulberry fruits can be processed to produce juice, which has potential applications in the food and beverage industry. Additionally, mulberry extracts can be utilized in the cosmetic and pharmaceutical industries due to their antioxidant and therapeutic properties.

Silkworm Waste

During the rearing of silkworms and the production of silk, various types of waste are generated, including:

Silkworm Litter: The excreta and exuviae (shed skins) of silkworms can be used as a rich source of organic fertilizer for agricultural purposes.

Pupal Waste: After the silk is extracted from the cocoons, the remaining pupal casings can be utilized in several ways:

- As a protein-rich animal feed supplement for poultry, fish, and livestock.

- As a source of valuable compounds like chitin, which has applications in the pharmaceutical and cosmetic industries.

- As a raw material for the production of silk sericin, a protein with potential applications in biomedicine and tissue engineering.

Silk Waste: Silk waste, including damaged cocoons, floss, and other silk fibers unsuitable for reeling, can be processed into spun silk yarns and fabrics. These materials find applications in the textile industry, as well as in the production of handicrafts and other value-added products.

Sericin Utilization

Sericin is a protein obtained from the silk glands of silkworms and is typically removed during the degumming process of silk production. Sericin has various applications, including:

Biomaterials and Tissue Engineering: Sericin can be used in the development of biomaterials for wound dressings, scaffolds for tissue engineering, and drug delivery systems due to its biocompatibility and biodegradability.

Cosmetics and Personal Care Products: Sericin possesses moisturizing, antioxidant, and anti-aging properties, making it a valuable ingredient in cosmetic formulations, such as creams, lotions, and hair care products.

Pharmaceuticals: Sericin exhibits potential therapeutic properties, including anti-inflammatory, antimicrobial, and antioxidant activities, making it a promising candidate for pharmaceutical applications.

Handicrafts and Value-Added Products

Sericulture byproducts can be utilized in the production of various handicrafts and value-added products, such as:

Silk Waste Yarns and Fabrics: Spun silk yarns and fabrics made from silk waste can be used in the production of garments, home furnishings, and other textile products.

Handicrafts: Damaged cocoons, silk waste, and other byproducts can be used to create decorative items, jewelry, and other handicrafts, providing additional income opportunities for artisans and entrepreneurs.

Biocomposites: Silk fibroin and sericin can be incorporated into biocomposites, enhancing their mechanical properties and biodegradability, with applications in various industries, including construction and automotive.

By effectively utilizing the byproducts of sericulture, the industry can not only reduce waste and environmental impact but also generate additional revenue streams, contribute to sustainable practices, and promote the development of innovative products across various sectors.

Chapter 7

Silkworm Seed Production

Grainage operations for the production of silkworm eggs

Grainage refers to the process of producing disease-free silkworm eggs on a commercial scale. It involves a series of steps starting from the selection of healthy silkworm breeds to the incubation and hatching of eggs. The main objective is to produce high quality silkworm eggs that are free from diseases like pebrine.

The key steps in grainage operations are:

Selection and preservation of seed cocoons

- Healthy silkworm breeds are selected based on traits like fecundity, viability of eggs, reelability of cocoons, etc.

- Seed cocoons are carefully chosen from the rearing lot and preserved under optimum conditions of temperature (25°C) and humidity (70-80%).

- The pupae inside the seed cocoons are allowed to develop into moths.

Emergence and coupling of moths

- The emerged male and female moths are allowed to mate for 3-4 hours.

- One male moth can be coupled with 1-2 females to maintain the vigor of the eggs.

Oviposition or egg laying

- After decoupling, the gravid female moths are kept in cellules for egg laying.

- Each moth lays around 400-500 eggs over a period of 24-48 hours.

- The egg sheets are then treated with 2% formalin solution for disinfection.

Mother moth examination

- After oviposition, the female moths are tested for the presence of pebrine spores by microscopic examination.

- If found infected, the entire egg batch laid by the moth is destroyed.

Acid treatment of eggs

- The eggs are treated with hydrochloric acid to break the diapause and initiate early hatching.

- This process also helps in surface sterilization of the eggs.

Incubation and hatching

- The acid treated eggs are washed and incubated at 25°C and 80% humidity for 10-12 days until hatching.

- The hatched silkworm larvae are then ready for brushing.

Throughout the grainage process, strict hygiene and sanitation measures are followed to prevent contamination. The grainage rooms and equipment are thoroughly disinfected before the operations. Only disease-free and robust eggs are supplied to the farmers for commercial rearing.

Some key points to ensure production of quality silkworm eggs in grainages are:

- Sourcing of pure and healthy silkworm breeds

- Proper preservation and care of seed cocoons

- Microscopic examination of mother moths to eliminate pebrine infected eggs

- Incubation of eggs under optimum conditions

- Timely supply of eggs to farmers synchronized with mulberry leaf availability

Grainage operations form the backbone of the sericulture industry. Production of high quality disease-free silkworm eggs is crucial for the success of silkworm rearing and eventual silk production. Grainages must adopt scientific methods and follow strict quality control measures to ensure a steady supply of superior silkworm eggs to the farmers.

Moth emergence, coupling and egg laying

Moth Emergence

After the silkworm larva spins its cocoon, it enters the pupal stage and undergoes metamorphosis to transform into an adult moth. This process takes about 10-14 days. The fully formed moth then secretes an alkaline fluid to soften one end of the cocoon and emerges by pushing its way out. Upon emergence, the moth appears wet and its wings are crumpled. It then climbs onto a surface, allows its wings to expand and dry, and expels a brownish fluid to clear its digestive system.

Some key points about moth emergence:

- Male moths tend to emerge earlier than females

- Newly emerged moths cannot fly as their wings are underdeveloped due to centuries of domestication

- Moths do not have functional mouthparts and do not feed during their short adult lifespan of 5-10 days

Coupling (Mating)

Silk moths begin searching for a mate almost immediately after emerging from their cocoons. Males are more active in this pursuit and rapidly flap their wings to attract females. Females release pheromones to signal their receptivity to mating.

The coupling process in silk moths involves:

- Male moths find and approach a female, then position themselves alongside her

- Copulation is initiated when the male clasps the female's abdomen with his claspers

- Mating pairs remain coupled for 3-4 hours, sometimes up to 6 hours

- Sperm is transferred from the male to the female's reproductive tract during coupling

- After mating, the female stores the sperm in a special receptacle to later fertilize her eggs

- Males can mate with 1-2 females but are usually rested for a few hours between matings to regain their vigor

- Females typically mate only once and then focus on egg-laying

Egg Laying (Oviposition)

After coupling, gravid female moths are kept in special trays or boxes for egg laying. This process is called oviposition. Each female can lay 300-500 eggs over a 24-48 hour period before dying.

Important aspects of the egg laying process:

- Eggs are deposited on specially made cards or paper in a uniform manner

- Ideal conditions for oviposition are 25°C temperature, 75-80% humidity, and semi-darkness

- Females cover the eggs with a gelatinous secretion that glues them to the substrate and protects them

- Egg color changes from yellow to gray/purple as they develop over 10-25 days

- Unfertilized eggs remain yellow and do not hatch

- Laid eggs must be microscopically examined to detect pebrine disease and discarded if infected

- Healthy eggs are then placed in cold storage or incubated for hatching into the next generation of silkworms

The moth stage completes the fascinating life cycle of the silkworm. Although the adult moths are flightless and short-lived, they play a crucial role in mating and producing hundreds of fertile eggs. Sericulture farms carefully manage the coupling and egg laying processes to ensure disease-free, high quality eggs for the next crop of silkworms. Proper environmental conditions and handling of moths are key to obtaining a good yield of silkworm eggs for continued silk production.

Cold storage and incubation of eggs

Cold storage of silkworm eggs is an important aspect of sericulture that enables the preservation of eggs and regulation of hatching time to match the availability of mulberry leaves for feeding. The main objectives of cold storage are:

- To prevent the eggs from entering diapause (hibernation) by storing them at low temperatures soon after laying

- To synchronize hatching of eggs based on the rearing schedule and leaf availability

- To preserve the eggs for longer durations (up to 10 months) for future use

The ideal conditions for cold storage of silkworm eggs are:

- Temperature: 2.5°C to 5°C

- Relative humidity: 70-80%

- Airtight containers to prevent desiccation of eggs

The eggs are usually refrigerated within 20-24 hours after oviposition to prevent diapause induction. The eggs can be stored in the following ways:

- Short-term storage: 2-3 days at 5°C to postpone hatching for a few days

- Medium-term storage: 15-30 days at 5°C for eggs laid in unfavorable seasons

- Long-term storage: Up to 10 months at 2.5°C for preservation of precious breeds or special purposes

The eggs are periodically checked for any signs of deterioration and the temperature and humidity conditions are strictly monitored during storage.

Incubation of Silkworm Eggs

Incubation refers to the process of providing suitable environmental conditions for the embryonic development and hatching of silkworm eggs. The success of silkworm rearing largely depends on the quality of incubation and the hatching percentage of eggs.

The optimum conditions for incubation of silkworm eggs are:

- Temperature: 25°C ± 1°C

- Relative humidity: 75-80%

- Photoperiod: 16 hours light and 8 hours darkness

- Good ventilation and hygiene

The steps involved in the incubation process are:

1. Acid treatment: The eggs are treated with dilute hydrochloric acid to break the diapause and initiate embryonic development. This is usually done for bivoltine breeds.

2. Black boxing: The acid treated eggs are kept in complete darkness for 48 hours at 25°C to ensure uniform development of the embryo.

3. Exposure to light: The eggs are then exposed to bright light (100 lux) for 2-3 days to promote uniform hatching.

4. Hatching: The eggs start hatching from the 10th day of incubation and continue for 2-3 days. The newly hatched larvae are then ready for brushing.

Some important precautions during incubation are:

- Avoid temperature fluctuations and maintain optimum humidity

- Prevent mechanical injury to the eggs during handling

- Maintain strict hygiene to avoid contamination and disease outbreak

- Provide good ventilation to prevent accumulation of carbon dioxide

- Ensure uniform hatching by providing adequate light exposure

Proper cold storage and incubation of silkworm eggs are crucial for the success of silkworm rearing. Cold storage helps in the long-term preservation of eggs and regulation of the rearing schedule, while incubation ensures the production of healthy and robust silkworm larvae. Sericulture farms must adopt scientific methods and maintain optimal environmental conditions during these processes to achieve high hatching percentage and crop yield.

Chapter 8

Non-Mulberry Sericulture

Non-mulberry sericulture, also known as wild or forest sericulture, involves the rearing of silkworms that feed on plants other than mulberry. While mulberry sericulture accounts for the bulk of global silk production, non-mulberry silks are unique and have their own distinct properties and appeal. India is the only country that produces all commercially important varieties of non-mulberry silks - tropical tasar, oak tasar, eri, and muga.

Types of Non-Mulberry Silks

1. Tasar Silk

Tasar silk is copperish in color and coarser than mulberry silk. It is mainly used for furnishings and interiors. Tasar silkworms, belonging to the genus Antheraea, thrive on the leaves of Asan, Arjun, Sal, and Oak trees. In India, tropical tasar is produced by the silkworm Antheraea mylitta in the states of Jharkhand, Chhattisgarh, Odisha, Maharashtra, West Bengal, and Andhra Pradesh. Oak tasar, a finer variety, is obtained from the silkworm *Antheraea proylei* in the sub-Himalayan belt covering Manipur, Himachal Pradesh, Uttarakhand, Assam, Meghalaya, and Jammu & Kashmir.

2. Eri Silk

Eri silk, also called **Endi or Errandi**, is a multivoltine silk spun from open-ended cocoons. It is creamy-white or brick-red in color. The domesticated Eri silkworm, *Samia ricini*, primarily feeds on castor leaves. Eri culture is practiced in the North-Eastern states of India, mainly Assam, Meghalaya, Manipur, Nagaland, and also in Bihar and West Bengal.

3. Muga Silk

Muga silk, the golden-yellow silk, is exclusive to Assam, India. It is obtained from the semi-domesticated multivoltine silkworm, *Antheraea assamensis*, which feeds on the aromatic leaves of **Som and Soalu plants**. Muga culture is an important cottage industry in Assam.

Advantages of Non-Mulberry Sericulture

- Provides livelihood to tribals and rural populations in forest areas

- Requires minimal investment as the silkworms feed on natural vegetation

- Eco-friendly as it helps in conservation of forests

- Each type of non-mulberry silk has unique properties and a niche market

- Huge potential as non-mulberry food plants are abundantly available in forests

Non-mulberry sericulture, though contributing to a small portion of the total silk production, is vital for preserving India's rich sericultural heritage. It provides a viable livelihood option for tribals and helps in the conservation of forests. With growing awareness about the uniqueness of non-mulberry silks and improved rearing practices, this sector has the potential to grow further and contribute significantly to the country's silk industry.

Rearing of wild silkworms like Tasar, Muga, Eri

Rearing of Tasar

Tasar silkworms (Antheraea mylitta) are wild silkworms that are commercially exploited in India for silk production. Unlike the domesticated mulberry silkworm (*Bombyx mori*) which is reared completely indoors, tasar silkworms are reared outdoors on host trees. This type of sericulture is known as wild or forest sericulture.

Host Plants for Tasar Silkworms

Tasar silkworms are polyphagous, meaning they feed on a variety of food plants. The primary host plants are:

- Arjun (***Terminalia arjuna)***

- Asan (***Terminalia tomentosa***)

- Sal (***Shorea robusta***)

Some secondary food plants include Phutuka (***Melastoma melabathricum***), Ber (***Zizyphus mauritiana***), Cashew (***Anacardium occidentale***), etc. The temperate tasar silkworm species ***Antheraea proylei*** feeds on different oak species (***Quercus spp.***).

Rearing Process

The rearing of tasar silkworms involves the following steps:

1. Egg stage: The tasar silkmoth lays eggs on the leaves of host trees. The eggs are incubated under natural conditions and hatch in about 7-10 days.

2. Early larval rearing: The newly hatched larvae are reared indoors for a short period and fed on fresh, tender leaves until they are robust enough to be placed on the host trees. This is done to ensure better survival of the young larvae.

3. Late larval rearing: The grown up larvae are then transferred to the host trees where they feed voraciously on the leaves. The rearers have to keep a watch on the larvae, protect them from predators, and sometimes transfer them to new trees when the leaves are completely consumed. The larval period lasts for 30-40 days.

4. Spinning: Once the larvae reach maturity, they start spinning cocoons on the branches of the host trees. The cocoons are harvested 7-10 days after spinning.

5. Reeling and processing: The harvested cocoons are then processed to extract the silk filament through reeling. Tasar cocoons are larger than mulberry cocoons and have a different reeling process.

Challenges in Tasar Sericulture

Rearing tasar silkworms in the wild comes with several challenges:

- Unpredictable weather conditions like heavy rains, cyclones, etc. can damage the host trees and the silkworms.

- Pests, predators and diseases are more difficult to control in outdoor conditions. Birds, ants, lizards, uzi flies, etc. can cause significant damage to the larvae.

- Proper management of the host trees in terms of pruning, fertilization, and protection from cattle grazing is necessary.

- Monitoring the larvae on tall trees is laborious and time consuming for the rearers.

- Lack of quality seed (eggs) and rearing technologies hampers the productivity.

Despite these challenges, tasar sericulture provides livelihood to many tribal communities in the tropical regions of India. Tasar silk, with its unique luster, texture and natural golden color, is a valuable product. Efforts are being made to improve the production and quality of tasar silk through better rearing practices and technological interventions.

The rearing of wild silkworms like tasar is quite different from mulberry sericulture. It requires working in harmony with nature, traditional ecological knowledge, and community participation. With increasing demand for wild silks, tasar sericulture has the potential to create sustainable income opportunities for forest-dependent communities while also conserving the natural ecosystems.

Rearing of Muga

Muga silkworm (*Antheraea assamensis*) is a semi-domesticated, multivoltine silkworm species endemic to Assam, India. It produces a unique golden-yellow silk known as Muga silk, which is highly prized for its glossy texture, durability and natural shimmering gold color. Muga silkworm rearing is an important traditional occupation for many communities in Assam.

Muga Silkworm Host Plants

Muga silkworms are polyphagous and feed on several host plants, primarily those belonging to the Lauraceae family. The two primary host plants are:

1. Som (*Persea bombycina*): It is the most preferred host plant, especially in upper Assam districts. Som leaves are highly nutritious for muga silkworms.

2. Soalu (*Litsea monopetala*): It is more common in lower Assam and foothill regions. Soalu is mainly used for young age rearing and seed crop rearing.

Some secondary host plants include Mejankari (*Litsea cubeba*), Digloti (*Litsea salicifolia*), Champa (*Michelia champaca*), etc. These are used during scarcity of primary host plants.

Rearing Process

Muga silkworms are reared outdoors on the host trees through 5-6 generations (broods) in a year. The rearing is conducted mainly in two commercial seasons:

- **Jethua (May-June):** Also called spring crop, it is the second most important commercial crop.

- Kotia (Oct-Nov): Known as autumn crop, it is the main commercial crop producing the best quality silk.

Other broods like Jarua, Chotua, Aherua, Bhodia are mainly used for seed production and maintenance.

The steps involved in muga silkworm rearing are:

1. Brushing: Newly hatched larvae are transferred to tender leaves on host trees.

2. Larval rearing: The silkworms are reared on host trees for 24-30 days, passing through 5 larval stages (instars). They molt 4 times, growing in size after each molt.

3. Mounting: Mature 5th instar larvae are transferred to mountages made of dry leaves and twigs (called jali) for cocooning.

4. Cocoon harvesting: Cocoons are harvested 7-10 days after mounting. Some cocoons are kept for seed production.

5. Seed production: Healthy cocoons are selected for producing eggs (seeds) for the next crop. Moths emerge from cocoons, mate and lay eggs which are incubated for the next brood.

Challenges in Muga Rearing

Muga silkworm rearing in outdoor conditions faces several challenges:

- Diseases like pebrine, flacherie, muscardine, etc. which can cause heavy crop losses

- Pests and predators like uzi fly, birds, ants, lizards that feed on silkworms

- Unfavorable weather conditions like heavy rains, storms, extreme temperatures

- Deforestation and shrinkage of host plant areas due to urbanization, expansion of tea gardens, etc.

- Lack of quality seeds and modern rearing technologies

- Price fluctuations and unorganized marketing of cocoons and silk

Despite these challenges, muga culture remains an integral part of Assam's heritage and rural economy. Efforts are being made to improve host plants, develop disease-resistant breeds, refine rearing practices and strengthen the seed and cocoon production systems to boost muga silk production.

The rearing of wild silkworms like muga is a unique and complex process that requires traditional ecological knowledge and community participation. With growing demand for this exotic silk, there is immense potential to promote muga culture as a sustainable livelihood option for the people of Assam while also conserving the biodiversity of the region.

Rearing of Eri

Eri silkworm (*Samia ricini*) is a domesticated silkworm species that is polyphagous in nature, meaning it can feed on a variety of host plants. It is reared primarily in the northeastern states of India like Assam, Meghalaya, Nagaland, Manipur, as well as in some parts of West Bengal and Bihar. Ericulture, or the practice of rearing Eri silkworms for silk production, is an important cottage industry in these regions.

Host Plants for Eri Silkworms

Eri silkworms can feed on several host plants, but the primary ones used for commercial rearing are:

- **Castor (*Ricinus communis*):** It is the most preferred host plant for Eri silkworms. Castor leaves are highly nutritious and result in good larval growth and cocoon yield.

- **Tapioca/Cassava (*Manihot esculenta*):** It is the second most important host plant, especially in regions where castor is not abundantly available.

- **Kesseru (*Heteropanax fragrans*):** A perennial plant used as a primary host in some areas.

Other secondary host plants include Ailanthus, Plumeria, Payam, Barpat, etc. The silkworms exhibit different growth and yield parameters when reared on different host plants.

Rearing Process

Eri silkworms are multivoltine, meaning they can be reared for 4-5 crops in a year. The rearing is done indoors, usually in the farmer's house or a separate rearing house. The steps involved are:

1. Egg stage: The Eri silkmoth lays 200-500 eggs which hatch in about 10 days. The eggs are incubated at 25-28°C and 80-90% humidity.

2. Brushing: The newly hatched larvae are carefully transferred to rearing trays containing fresh, tender leaves using a soft brush. This process is called brushing.

3. Larval rearing: The silkworms are fed with chopped leaves 4-5 times a day. They undergo 4 moults and 5 larval stages (instars). The larval period lasts for 20-30 days.

4. Spinning: The mature 5th instar larvae stop feeding and start spinning silk to form the cocoon. Eri silkworms are unique in that they spin open-ended cocoons unlike other silkworms. The spinning takes 2-3 days.

5. Harvesting cocoons: The cocoons are harvested 7-8 days after spinning. They are open-ended and are hand-spun into silk yarn instead of reeling.

6. Seed production: Some cocoons are allowed to develop into moths for breeding. The moths emerge in 10-14 days, mate, and lay eggs for the next crop.

Throughout the rearing, optimum temperature (25-28°C), humidity (80-90%), hygiene, and adequate feeding are critical for good cocoon yield.

Advantages of Ericulture

- Provides additional income to farmers from a short duration crop

- Can be practiced indoors with minimal investment

- Eri silk is strong, durable and has thermal properties making it valuable

- Byproducts like pupae are a good source of protein for poultry/fish feed

- Helps in women empowerment as it is mostly carried out by women

Challenges in Ericulture

- Diseases like pebrine, flacherie, muscardine can cause crop losses

- Fluctuations in cocoon price and lack of organized marketing

- Shortage of quality silkworm eggs (seeds)

- Lack of scientific rearing practices among some farmers

Despite the challenges, Eri culture remains an important livelihood activity for many rural families in the northeastern states of India. Efforts are being made by the Central Silk Board and state governments to promote Ericulture through improved host plants, better rearing techniques, and supporting seed production and cocoon marketing. With growing demand for Eri silk, there is good potential for this industry to grow further and benefit the farmers.

Properties and uses of non-mulberry silk

Properties of Tasar Silk

Tasar silk, also known as tussar, tussah or kosa silk, is a type of wild silk that possesses several unique properties:

1. Texture and appearance:

- Tasar silk has a rich, coarse texture compared to the smoother mulberry silk. This gives it a unique, slightly rough feel.

- It has a natural deep gold or copper-like color and a dull sheen, unlike the bright luster of mulberry silk.

- The silk fibers are shorter and not as fine as mulberry silk, resulting in a more uneven surface and slubby appearance.

2. Strength and durability:

- Despite its coarse texture, tasar silk is known for its high strength and durability.

- The presence of long chain amino acids and hydrogen bonds in the silk protein contributes to its superior mechanical properties.

- Tasar silk has higher tensile strength, toughness and elongation compared to mulberry silk, both in dry and wet conditions.

3. Thermal properties:

- Tasar silk is cool and breathable, making it suitable for warm climates.

- The silk has good insulation properties, keeping the wearer warm in winter and cool in summer.

- Its porous structure allows better air circulation and moisture wicking compared to other silks.

4. Comfort and drape:

- Tasar silk is lightweight and has a good drape, allowing it to fall gracefully.

- Despite the coarse texture, it feels soft and luxurious against the skin.

- The silk is hypoallergenic and does not cause skin irritation.

5. Dyeability:

- Tasar silk can be dyed in a wide range of colors, from natural earthy tones to bright hues.

- However, the natural golden color is often retained and used as a base for designing textiles.

- The dyed fabric may have a dual-tone effect due to the uneven surface and slubby texture.

Uses of Tasar Silk

Tasar silk's unique properties make it suitable for various applications:

1. Clothing and accessories:

- Tasar silk is popularly used for making sarees, especially in India. The sarees often feature intricate motifs and designs that complement the natural texture of the silk.

- It is also used for making suits, dresses, kurtis, stoles, dupattas and other garments.

- Tasar silk scarves, shawls and ties are appreciated for their rich look and feel.

2. Home furnishings:

- Tasar silk is used for making curtains, drapes, upholstery and wall hangings.

- Cushion covers, throw pillows and bedding made from tasar silk add a luxurious touch to home decor.

- The silk's natural resistance to dirt and odor makes it suitable for furnishings.

3. Handicrafts:

- Tasar silk is used in various handicrafts like paintings, wall hangings, showpieces etc.

- Its texture and natural golden color provide an attractive base for artistic works.

- In Odisha, tasar silk is used for the traditional pattachitra paintings.

4. Quilts and blankets:

- Tasar silk's good insulation properties make it ideal for quilts and blankets.

- The silk provides warmth without adding bulk, resulting in lightweight yet cozy quilts.

5. Soap and cosmetics:

- Tasar silk fiber is sometimes used as an exfoliant in handmade soaps and scrubs.

- Silk peptides derived from tasar silk are used in cosmetic products for their moisturizing and anti-aging properties.

Tasar silk's unique blend of strength, comfort, texture and natural beauty makes it a sought-after material for both clothing and home furnishings. Its adaptability to various design and craft techniques further enhances its value and versatility. From luxurious sarees to cozy quilts, tasar silk adds a touch of elegance and artisanal charm to any product it is used in.

Properties of Muga Silk

Muga silk, produced only in Assam, India, is one of the rarest and most valuable silks in the world. It is obtained from the semi-domesticated silkworm *Antheraea assamensis*. Muga silk has several unique properties that set it apart from other silks:

1. Natural golden color:

- Muga silk has a distinct glossy golden-yellow color that is entirely natural.

- The color is due to the presence of carotenoids in the silk fibers.

- The golden hue is so inherent that muga silk cannot be bleached or dyed easily.

2. High luster and sheen:

- Muga silk has a beautiful shimmering sheen and luster that increases with each wash.

- The triangular prism-like structure of the silk fibers allows them to reflect light at different angles, creating the lustrous effect.

3. Strength and durability:

- Muga silk is known as one of the strongest natural fibers.

- It has excellent tensile strength, toughness and elasticity compared to mulberry silk.

- Muga silk fabrics are said to outlast their wearer, retaining their qualities for years.

4. Texture and comfort:

- Muga silk has a smooth, soft texture that is comfortable against the skin.

- It is less smooth and more coarse compared to mulberry silk due to the presence of more sericin gum.

- The unique texture lends a rich, exotic feel to muga silk products.

5. Moisture-wicking and breathability:

- Muga silk is breathable and has good moisture-wicking properties.

- It can absorb up to 30-40% of its weight in moisture without feeling damp.

- This makes muga silk suitable for warm and humid climates.

6. Hypoallergenic and anti-bacterial:

- Muga silk is a natural protein fiber that is hypoallergenic and resistant to mold, fungus and bacteria.

- It does not cause skin irritation and is suitable for people with sensitive skin.

7. UV resistance:

- Muga silk provides good protection against ultraviolet rays compared to other silks and fibers.

- This makes it apt for use in sun umbrellas and outdoor clothing.

Uses of Muga Silk

The unique properties and rich appearance of muga silk make it valuable for various applications:

1. Traditional attire:

- In Assam, muga silk is traditionally used to make mekhela chadors, rihas and sadors for women.

- Men's clothing like dhotis, kurtas and headgear are also made from muga silk.

- Muga silk garments are considered a status symbol and are worn for festive occasions and rituals.

2. Fashion and accessories:

- Muga silk is used to create exquisite sarees, stoles, scarves, ties and other fashion accessories.

- Designers use muga silk fabric for high-end ethnic and fusion wear collections.

- Muga silk's natural golden color and luster enhance the richness of the garments.

3. Home furnishings:

- The strength and durability of muga silk make it ideal for home décor products.

- Curtains, draperies, cushion covers, quilts and wall hangings made from muga silk add a touch of luxury.

- Muga silk's resistance to dirt and odor is an advantage in furnishings.

4. Cosmetics and skincare:

- Hydrolyzed muga silk protein is used in cosmetic formulations for its film-forming and moisturizing properties.

- It helps reduce transepidermal water loss and keeps skin hydrated, thus reducing the appearance of fine lines.

- Skincare products with muga silk extracts are used for anti-aging and skin rejuvenation.

5. Handicrafts and souvenirs:

- Muga silk's exclusivity makes it a sought-after material for handicrafts and gift items.

- Paintings, wall hangings, decorative boxes and jewellery made with muga silk are popular souvenirs.

Muga silk's exceptional qualities - the golden luster, strength, smoothness and hypoallergenic nature - make it one of the most prized silks globally. Its value is enhanced by the limited production capacity and the traditional skills required to rear the silkworms and weave the silk. From luxurious garments to anti-aging cosmetics, muga silk's versatility and timeless appeal ensure its continued use and significance in the future.

Properties of Eri Silk

Eri silk, also known as Ahimsa silk or peace silk, is a unique silk variety produced by the domesticated Eri silkworm, Samia ricini. It has several distinctive properties that set it apart from other silks:

1. Texture and appearance:

- Eri silk has a soft, woolly texture due to its short staple length and spinning process.

- It has a matte appearance with a subtle sheen, unlike the high luster of mulberry silk.

- The silk has a natural off-white or creamy color.

2. Strength and durability:

- Eri silk is known for its exceptional strength and durability compared to other silks.

- The silk fibers have good tensile strength, making the fabric resistant to wear and tear.

- Eri silk products are known to last for generations with proper care.

3. Thermal properties:

- Eri silk is an excellent insulator, providing warmth in cold weather.

- It also has good breathability and moisture-wicking properties, making it comfortable to wear in warm weather.

- The silk's unique thermal properties make it suitable for all-season use.

4. Comfort and drape:

- Eri silk fabrics have a soft, smooth feel against the skin.

- The silk has good draping properties, falling gracefully and elegantly.

- It is lightweight and comfortable to wear.

5. Hypoallergenic and eco-friendly:

- Eri silk is naturally hypoallergenic, making it suitable for people with sensitive skin.

- The silk is produced without the use of harsh chemicals, making it an eco-friendly choice.

- Eri silk production is considered cruelty-free as the silkworms are allowed to emerge from their cocoons before the silk is harvested.

6. Blending properties:

- Eri silk fibers blend well with other natural fibers like cotton, wool, and cashmere.

- Blending enhances the properties of the final fabric, such as softness, drape, and durability.

Uses of Eri Silk

The unique properties of Eri silk make it suitable for a wide range of applications:

1. Clothing:

- Eri silk is commonly used to make traditional garments like sarees, shawls, and stoles.

- It is also used for making contemporary clothing like dresses, skirts, and tops.

- Eri silk's thermal properties make it ideal for winter wear like jackets and coats.

2. Home furnishings:

- Eri silk is used to make luxurious home textiles like curtains, drapes, and upholstery.

- Bedding products like sheets, pillowcases, and duvets made from Eri silk provide comfort and insulation.

- The silk's durability makes it suitable for high-use items like cushion covers and throw pillows.

3. Accessories:

- Eri silk is used to make fashionable accessories like scarves, stoles, and neckties.

- Its softness and drape make it ideal for making elegant evening wear accessories.

4. Baby products:

- Eri silk's hypoallergenic properties make it suitable for making baby clothing and bedding.

- The silk's softness and breathability ensure comfort for delicate baby skin.

5. Textile art and handicrafts:

- Eri silk's natural texture and color make it a popular choice for textile art and handicrafts.

- It is used for making wall hangings, tapestries, and decorative items.

- Eri silk's blending properties allow for creative combinations with other fibers in handcrafted products.

Eri silk's unique combination of strength, durability, comfort, and eco-friendliness make it a valuable and versatile silk variety. Its thermal properties, hypoallergenic nature, and luxurious feel make it suitable for a wide range of clothing, home furnishing, and accessory applications. As a cruelty-free and sustainable silk option, Eri silk is gaining popularity among environmentally conscious consumers worldwide. The increasing demand for Eri silk products is also supporting the livelihoods of the communities involved in its production, particularly in the North-Eastern states of India.

Chapter 9

Sericulture Economics and Marketing

Economics of mulberry and cocoon production

Economics of Mulberry Cultivation

Mulberry is the sole food plant for the silkworm *Bombyx mori* and its cultivation forms the foundation for the sericulture industry. The economics of mulberry cultivation involves various costs and returns.

Establishment Costs

Establishing a new mulberry garden involves several one-time costs such as:

- Land preparation (ploughing, leveling, etc.)

- Digging pits and planting mulberry saplings

- Cost of saplings

- Manures and fertilizers

- Irrigation setup

- Fencing and other miscellaneous costs

The establishment costs can range from Rs. 15,000 to Rs. 20,000 per acre, with planting material and manures constituting major expenses.

Recurring Costs

From the second year onwards, the recurring costs in mulberry cultivation include:

- Manures and fertilizers

- Irrigation

- Weeding and hoeing

- Pruning and training

- Leaf harvesting and transportation

- Plant protection measures

- Land revenue and other taxes

The annual recurring costs can vary from Rs. 25,000 to Rs. 35,000 per acre depending on the intensity of cultivation and local conditions.

Leaf Yield and Returns

A well-maintained mulberry garden can yield about 12-15 tons of leaves per acre per year from the third year onwards. The leaf yield depends on factors like variety, spacing, inputs, and management practices.

The gross returns from mulberry cultivation is calculated by multiplying the leaf yield with the prevailing market price of mulberry leaves. The net returns is arrived at by deducting the recurring costs from the gross returns.

On an average, the net returns from an acre of mulberry garden ranges from Rs. 30,000 to Rs. 50,000 per year. However, most sericulture farmers utilize the mulberry leaves for rearing their own silkworms rather than selling them.

Economics of Cocoon Production

Cocoon production involves rearing silkworms by feeding them with mulberry leaves and facilitating them to spin cocoons. The economics of cocoon production depends on several factors.

Fixed Costs

The fixed costs in cocoon production include:

- Rearing shed construction and maintenance

- Rearing equipment (trays, nets, mountages, etc.)

- Depreciation and interest on fixed capital

The fixed costs are usually spread over several years and constitute a minor portion of the total costs.

Variable Costs

The major variable costs in cocoon production are:

- Cost of silkworm eggs (layings)

- Cost of mulberry leaves

- Labor charges for brushing, feeding, cleaning, mounting, etc.

- Cost of disinfectants and other chemicals

- Electricity and other utilities

The variable costs contribute to 70-80% of the total costs in cocoon production.

Cocoon Yield and Returns

The cocoon yield per 100 Disease Free Layings (DFLs) ranges from 60-80 kg depending on the silkworm breed, season, and rearing practices. The cocoon price varies based on the quality and market demand.

The gross returns is calculated by multiplying the cocoon yield with the market price. The net returns is obtained by deducting the total costs from the gross returns.

On an average, the net returns from rearing 100 DFLs ranges from Rs. 5,000 to Rs. 8,000. Rearing 300-400 DFLs per batch is considered an economically viable unit.

Factors Affecting Profitability

The profitability of sericulture depends on several inter-related factors:

- Mulberry leaf yield and quality

- Silkworm breed and quality of layings

- Rearing management and cocoon yield

- Market price of cocoons and raw silk

- Government support and subsidies

- Availability of timely credit

- Skill and experience of the sericulture farmer

Efficient utilization of resources, adoption of improved technologies, effective disease management, and collective marketing are some of the ways to enhance the profitability of sericulture.

The economics of mulberry cultivation and cocoon production varies across regions and seasons. While the establishment costs are high, the recurring costs are relatively lower. The net returns depend on the productivity levels and market prices. Sericulture, being a labor-intensive and rural-based activity, provides gainful employment and income to millions of farmers, particularly in the tropical regions. Governmental support through subsidies, infrastructure, and extension services plays a crucial role in the economics of sericulture.

Marketing channels for cocoons and raw silk

Cocoon Marketing Channels

Cocoon markets serve as the primary link between silkworm rearers and reelers. The main marketing channels for cocoons are:

1. Government Cocoon Markets: These markets are operated by the state sericulture departments or silk boards. They ensure fair prices, quality control, and transparency in transactions. The famous Ramanagara Cocoon Market in Karnataka is Asia's largest, where 40,000 to 50,000 kg of cocoons are traded daily.

2. Private Reelers: Many reelers directly procure cocoons from rearers to ensure quality and control costs. However, prices may vary and rearers have less bargaining power in this channel.

3. Cooperative Societies: Some rearers sell their cocoons to cooperative societies which in turn supply to reelers or government agencies. This channel offers better prices than private reelers.

4. Mahajans and Middlemen: Local money lenders (mahajans) and middlemen (paikars) are informal but significant players in cocoon trade. They offer quick cash to rearers but at lower prices compared to government rates.

The price of cocoons varies across channels, with government markets offering the highest, followed by cooperatives, private reelers, and middlemen. The quality and breed of cocoons also determine the price.

Raw Silk Marketing Channels

The main marketing channels for raw silk are:

1. Government Agencies: Central Silk Board (CSB) and state silk boards are the major buyers of raw silk. They procure silk from reelers and maintain buffer stocks to stabilize prices.

2. Cooperative Societies: Many reelers sell their raw silk to cooperative societies which have tie-ups with weavers' cooperatives and government agencies. This ensures a steady market and fair prices for reelers.

3. Private Weavers and Traders: A significant portion of raw silk is sold directly to private weavers and traders who offer competitive prices. However, this channel is unorganized and lacks quality control.

4. Exports: India exports 20-30% of its raw silk, mainly to Europe and the USA. The CSB and private exporters buy silk from reelers and sell in the global market.

The price of raw silk depends on the grade (2A, 3A, 4A etc.), denier (thickness), and type (mulberry, tasar, eri, muga). Government rates are usually higher than private channels.

Challenges in Cocoon and Raw Silk Marketing

Despite the organized marketing system, the cocoon and raw silk trade faces several challenges:

- Price fluctuations due to demand-supply mismatch and speculation

- Quality inconsistency and lack of grading standards

- Delayed payments and credit issues for reelers and rearers

- Inadequate storage and logistics infrastructure

- Competition from imported silk, especially from China

To address these issues, the government is taking steps like e-trading of cocoons, quality certification, price stabilization, and branding of Indian silk. Reelers are being encouraged to adopt best practices and upgrade technology to improve productivity and quality.

The marketing channels for cocoons and raw silk in India are diverse, with both organized and unorganized players. While government agencies play a key role in ensuring fair prices and quality, private channels offer competitive rates and flexibility. Strengthening the marketing infrastructure, quality control, and value addition are crucial for the sustainable growth of the Indian silk industry. Improving the efficiency and transparency of cocoon and raw silk markets can boost the incomes of silkworm rearers and reelers, and help India compete in the global silk market.

Sericulture as a rural industry for employment and income generation

Sericulture, the production of silk through rearing of silkworms, is an important agro-based rural cottage industry in India. It provides gainful employment and income generation opportunities to millions of rural households, particularly small and marginal farmers, landless labourers, and women. Sericulture is a labour-intensive industry that requires low capital investment and offers high returns, making it an attractive option for rural development.

Employment Generation Potential

Sericulture involves a series of activities from mulberry cultivation to silk fabric production, each creating employment at various stages:

1. Mulberry cultivation: Planting, pruning, fertilizing, irrigating, and harvesting mulberry leaves.

2. Silkworm rearing: Raising silkworms from eggs to cocoons by feeding them mulberry leaves.

3. Silk reeling: Unwinding silk filaments from cocoons and twisting them into yarn.

4. Silk weaving: Weaving silk yarn into fabrics using handlooms or power looms.

5. Other activities: Silk printing, dyeing, finishing, and marketing.

It is estimated that sericulture can generate employment of 11 man-days per kg of raw silk production (in on-farm and off-farm activities) throughout the year. One hectare of mulberry creates year-round employment for about 12-13 people. Sericulture is currently practiced in about 52,360 villages across India, providing livelihood to around 7.56 million people, most of them being small and marginal farmers and rural artisans.

Income Generation Potential

Sericulture provides a steady source of income to rural families as it can be practiced 4-6 times a year, unlike most agricultural crops which provide income only once or twice a year. The income from sericulture is estimated to be 5-6 times higher than that from agricultural crops.

A study in Kharasia block of Chhattisgarh found that most sericulture farmers earned Rs. 5000 to Rs. 15000 per annum from cocoon production. Another study in Dharamjaigarh block of Chhattisgarh reported that sericulture contributed 25-30% to the total income of practicing households.

Silk reeling and weaving activities further enhance the income of rural artisans. The high value of silk and its global demand ensure remunerative prices for the producers.

Women Empowerment

Sericulture is a women-friendly occupation as most of its activities are home-based and can be done along with household chores. About 60% of the labor force in sericulture is constituted by women. Silkworm rearing is particularly suitable for women as it requires patience, care, and attention to detail.

Engaging in sericulture gives women an opportunity to earn an independent income, contribute to household finances, and enhance their decision-making power. It boosts their self-confidence and social status in the community.

Advantages as a Rural Industry

1. Provides employment and income in rural areas, reducing migration to cities.

2. Suits landless farmers as silkworm rearing can be done indoors with little land.

3. Requires low capital investment and offers quick returns.

4. Eco-friendly activity as it involves no use of chemical fertilizers or pesticides.

5. Preserves traditional skills and cultural heritage of silk production.

6. Has potential for value addition and product diversification.

Challenges and Way Forward

Despite its immense potential, the sericulture industry in India faces some challenges:

- Fluctuations in cocoon and silk prices

- Inadequate quality control and grading mechanisms

- Insufficient access to improved technologies and training

- Lack of proper forward and backward linkages

- Competition from cheap imported silk, especially from China

To tap the full potential of sericulture for rural employment and income generation, there is a need for:

- Strengthening research and development for high-yielding silkworm breeds and mulberry varieties

- Providing quality silkworm eggs, rearing equipment, and reeling machinery to farmers at subsidized rates

- Imparting training on scientific rearing practices and post-cocoon processes

- Establishing common facility centers for reeling, twisting, and weaving

- Developing effective marketing channels and value chains

- Promoting silk as an eco-friendly and ethical fabric in domestic and international markets

Sericulture is a promising rural industry that can provide sustainable livelihoods to millions of people in India. With the right policies, investments, and institutional support, sericulture can become a key driver of inclusive rural development and poverty alleviation in the country.

Chapter 10

Recent Advances and Future of Sericulture

Application of biotechnology in host plant and silkworm improvement

Biotechnology has emerged as a powerful tool to complement conventional breeding methods for the genetic improvement of both mulberry and silkworm, the two key components of sericulture. Advances in tissue culture, molecular markers, genetic engineering and omics technologies are being harnessed to develop superior mulberry varieties and silkworm breeds.

Biotechnology for Mulberry Improvement

Tissue Culture and Micropropagation

- Micropropagation protocols have been standardized for rapid multiplication of elite mulberry genotypes. This ensures production of true-to-type, disease-free planting material round the year.

- Somatic embryogenesis and synthetic seed technology are being used for mass propagation and germplasm conservation of mulberry.

Molecular Markers

- Various DNA markers like RAPD, ISSR, AFLP, SSR etc. have been developed for mulberry genetic diversity analysis, germplasm characterization, and construction of linkage maps.

- Marker-assisted selection (MAS) is being employed for precise and accelerated breeding of mulberry for traits like stress tolerance, disease resistance and leaf quality.

Genetic Engineering

- Protocols for mulberry transformation using Agrobacterium have been optimized. Genes for abiotic stress tolerance (HVA1, DREB, osmotin etc.), biotic stress resistance (Bt toxin, chitinase etc.) and leaf quality improvement have been introduced in mulberry.

- Notably, transgenic mulberry expressing the barley HVA1 gene showed enhanced tolerance to drought, salt and cold stresses. Field trials of these transgenics are underway.

Functional Genomics and Omics

- The draft genome of mulberry has been sequenced which will aid in the discovery of genes/QTLs governing important agronomic traits.

- Transcriptomics, proteomics and metabolomics are being used to decipher the molecular basis of stress tolerance, disease resistance and leaf quality in mulberry.

- Genome editing tools like CRISPR/Cas are likely to be employed for precise modification of target genes in mulberry in future.

Biotechnology for Silkworm Improvement

Molecular Markers

- Silkworm genomic resources like EST libraries, linkage maps, and genome sequence are available. These are being utilized to identify DNA markers linked to genes/QTLs controlling commercially important traits.

- MAS is being used for the development of silkworm breeds with higher productivity, better silk quality, tolerance to biotic and abiotic stresses, etc.

Transgenesis

- Efficient methods for silkworm transgenesis using piggyBac transposon and CRISPR/Cas9 have been developed.

- Transgenic silkworms expressing fluorescent proteins in the silk gland produce colored silks. Those expressing spider silk genes produce stronger and more elastic silk fibers.

- Silkworms are also being explored as bioreactors for production of recombinant proteins of biomedical and industrial importance in the silk glands.

Genome Editing

- CRISPR/Cas9 system is being employed for targeted mutagenesis of silkworm genes to elucidate their functions.

- This technology is also being used to create knock-out mutants for disease resistance. For example, knocking out the receptor genes for BmNPV resulted in silkworms highly resistant to viral infection.

Omics and Systems Biology

- Whole genome sequencing of silkworm has been achieved. Transcriptomics, proteomics and metabolomics are being integrated to get a systems-level understanding of silkworm biology.

- This knowledge will help in the design of superior silkworm strains through modern breeding or genetic engineering approaches.

The application of biotechnology in sericulture has opened up new avenues for the development of improved host plant and silkworm varieties. Integrating these modern tools with conventional breeding will accelerate the vertical growth of sericulture industry. However, the genetically modified mulberry and silkworm varieties need to be rigorously evaluated for their safety and environmental impact before deployment in the field. Capacity building and effective regulatory mechanisms are also essential for harnessing the full potential of biotechnology in sericulture improvement.

Biomedical applications of silk proteins

Silk proteins, particularly silk fibroin derived from the cocoons of the domesticated silkworm *Bombyx mori*, have emerged as promising biomaterials for a wide range of biomedical applications. The unique properties of silk fibroin, including its biocompatibility, biodegradability, mechanical robustness, and versatile processability, make it an attractive candidate for various medical uses.

Tissue Engineering and Regenerative Medicine

One of the most promising applications of silk fibroin is in the field of tissue engineering and regenerative medicine. Silk fibroin can be processed into various formats such as films, hydrogels, sponges, and nanofibers that serve as scaffolds to support cell adhesion, proliferation, and differentiation.

Some key applications include:

- **Bone tissue engineering:** Silk fibroin scaffolds, alone or in combination with other materials like hydroxyapatite, have been used to regenerate bone defects. The scaffolds provide mechanical support and guide the growth of new bone tissue.

- **Cartilage repair:** Porous silk fibroin sponges and hydrogels have been explored as matrices for cartilage tissue engineering. They support the growth of chondrocytes and promote the formation of cartilaginous extracellular matrix.

- **Skin wound healing:** Silk fibroin films and electrospun nanofibrous mats have been used as wound dressings to promote skin regeneration. They provide a moist environment, allow oxygen permeability, and support re-epithelialization.

- **Vascular grafts:** Silk fibroin has been investigated for the fabrication of small-diameter vascular grafts. The mechanical strength and blood compatibility of silk make it suitable for this application.

- Ligament and tendon repair: Braided or knitted silk fibroin scaffolds have the potential to regenerate ligaments and tendons by providing mechanical support and guiding tissue growth.

Drug Delivery

Silk fibroin has also been widely explored as a drug delivery vehicle due to its controllable degradation, biocompatibility, and ability to stabilize labile compounds. Various silk-based drug delivery systems have been developed:

- Silk nanoparticles: Drugs can be encapsulated within silk fibroin nanoparticles for targeted and sustained delivery. The particles protect the drugs and allow controlled release at the desired site.

- Silk hydrogels: Therapeutic agents like small molecule drugs, proteins, and growth factors can be loaded into silk hydrogels. The hydrogels provide a sustained release profile and can be injected for localized delivery.

- Silk films and coatings: Drugs can be incorporated into silk fibroin films or coated onto medical implants for localized and sustained delivery. This approach is useful for preventing infections and enhancing tissue integration.

- Silk-based gene delivery: Silk fibroin has been used to deliver genes and siRNA for gene therapy applications. The silk carriers protect the nucleic acids and facilitate cellular uptake.

Other Biomedical Applications

Apart from tissue engineering and drug delivery, silk fibroin has found use in several other biomedical domains:

- **Biomedical sensors:** Silk fibroin's optical transparency and flexibility make it suitable for fabricating biocompatible and implantable sensors for monitoring physiological parameters.

- **Bioelectronics:** Silk fibroin has been used as a substrate and dielectric material for flexible and biodegradable electronics that can interface with the body.

- **Ophthalmology:** Silk fibroin has been explored for corneal repair, ocular drug delivery, and as a material for contact lenses.

- **Plastic surgery:** Silk fibroin has potential as a dermal filler for soft tissue augmentation due to its biocompatibility and longevity.

Silk fibroin from silkworms is a versatile biomaterial platform with immense potential in various biomedical applications. Its unique properties, along with the ability to process it into diverse formats, have led to its use in tissue engineering, regenerative medicine, drug delivery, and other medical fields. As research continues to advance, it is expected that silk-based biomaterials will play an increasingly important role in improving patient outcomes and quality of life. However, further studies are needed to address challenges such as immunogenicity, batch-to-batch variability, and large-scale production before widespread clinical translation can be achieved.

Challenges and future prospects of the sericulture industry

Challenges Faced by the Sericulture Industry

The sericulture industry, despite its economic importance and potential, faces several challenges that hinder its growth and sustainability. Some of the major challenges are:

1. Diseases and pests:

- Silkworms are susceptible to various diseases like pebrine, flacherie, grasserie, and muscardine, which can cause significant crop losses.

- Pests like uzi fly, dermestid beetles, and vertebrate predators also pose a threat to silkworm rearing.

- Lack of proper disease and pest management practices among farmers exacerbates the problem.

2. Fluctuations in cocoon and raw silk prices:

- The prices of cocoons and raw silk are highly volatile due to demand-supply mismatches and speculation.

- Price instability affects the profitability and livelihood of sericulture farmers and reelers.

- Absence of effective price stabilization mechanisms and market linkages aggravate the issue.

3. Climate change and weather vagaries:

- Sericulture is highly sensitive to climatic conditions like temperature, humidity, and rainfall.

- Extreme weather events, prolonged droughts, and erratic rainfall patterns due to climate change adversely affect mulberry leaf production and silkworm rearing.

- Lack of climate-resilient mulberry varieties and silkworm breeds make the industry vulnerable.

4. Inadequate quality control and grading:

- Absence of strict quality control measures and grading standards for cocoons and raw silk leads to inconsistency in quality.

- Poor quality affects the marketability and price realization of the produce.

- Lack of quality testing facilities and trained personnel hinder quality improvement efforts.

5. Outdated technology and infrastructure:

- Many sericulture farmers still rely on traditional methods and equipment for silkworm rearing, reeling, and weaving.

- Outdated technology results in low productivity, high production costs, and poor quality of output.

- Inadequate infrastructure facilities like rearing sheds, reeling units, and storage rooms affect the efficiency of operations.

6. Competition from synthetic fibers and imported silk:

- The increasing popularity of low-cost synthetic fibers like polyester and nylon has reduced the demand for silk.

- Cheap imported silk, especially from China, has flooded the domestic market, making it difficult for Indian silk to compete.

- Lack of product diversification and value addition has limited the market opportunities for Indian silk.

7. Socio-economic constraints:

- Sericulture is largely practiced by small and marginal farmers who lack access to credit, technology, and market information.

- Low literacy levels and lack of entrepreneurial skills among sericulture farmers hinder their ability to adopt modern practices and explore new markets.

- Migration of rural youth to urban areas for better employment opportunities has led to labor shortages in sericulture.

Future Prospects of the Sericulture Industry

Despite the challenges, the sericulture industry has immense potential for growth and development in the future. Some of the promising prospects are:

1. Growing demand for natural and sustainable fibers:

- There is a rising global consciousness about the environmental impact of synthetic fibers, leading to a renewed interest in natural fibers like silk.

- Silk, being a biodegradable and eco-friendly fiber, is well-positioned to cater to the growing demand for sustainable fashion and textiles.

- The unique properties of silk, such as its luster, drape, and comfort, make it a preferred choice for high-end and luxury products.

2. Expansion of non-textile applications:

- Apart from traditional textile uses, silk proteins are finding novel applications in the biomedical, cosmetic, and food industries.

- Silk fibroin is being explored for tissue engineering, drug delivery, and wound healing due to its biocompatibility and controlled degradation properties.

- Silk peptides are used in cosmetic formulations for their moisturizing and anti-aging benefits.

- Silk powder is used as a functional food ingredient and dietary supplement.

3. Technological advancements and innovations:

- Application of biotechnology, such as marker-assisted selection and genetic engineering, can lead to the development of high-yielding, disease-resistant mulberry varieties and silkworm breeds.

- Adoption of advanced rearing techniques like chawki rearing, shoot rearing, and round-the-year rearing can increase the productivity and profitability of sericulture.

- Innovations in reeling and weaving technologies, like automatic reeling machines and power looms, can improve the efficiency and quality of silk production.

4. Diversification and value addition:

- Diversification of silk products beyond traditional sarees and dress materials, into items like home furnishings, accessories, and technical textiles, can open up new market avenues.

- Value addition through designing, printing, dyeing, and finishing can enhance the appeal and marketability of silk products.

- Promotion of organic and Ahimsa (non-violent) silk can cater to the niche market of ethical and conscious consumers.

5. Institutional support and policy initiatives:

- Government schemes like Silk Samagra and North East Region Textile Promotion Scheme (NERTPS) provide financial and technical assistance for the holistic development of the sericulture industry.

- Establishment of sericulture clusters, common facility centers, and silk parks can promote entrepreneurship and generate employment opportunities.

- Strengthening of research and development institutions, extension services, and capacity building programs can improve the knowledge and skills of sericulture stakeholders.

6. Promotion of sericulture tourism:

- Sericulture, with its rich cultural heritage and picturesque mulberry fields, has the potential to attract tourists interested in agro-tourism and eco-tourism.

- Promotion of sericulture tourism can generate additional income for farmers and create awareness about the industry among the public.

- Integration of sericulture with other tourism activities like handicraft demonstrations, silk weaving workshops, and farm stays can provide a unique experience to visitors.

While the sericulture industry faces multiple challenges, it also has promising prospects for growth and diversification. Addressing the challenges through technological interventions, policy support, and market-oriented strategies can help realize the full potential of the industry. Sericulture, with its capacity to generate employment, empower women, and promote sustainable development, can continue to play a vital role in the socio-economic fabric of the country. A concerted effort from all stakeholders - farmers, reelers, weavers, researchers, policymakers, and entrepreneurs - is needed to take the Indian sericulture industry to new heights in the future.

Chapter 11

Sericulture Machinery and Equipment

Types of equipment used in mulberry cultivation

Mulberry cultivation involves various activities like land preparation, planting, pruning, harvesting, etc. Different types of equipment and machinery are used to carry out these operations efficiently. The choice of equipment depends on the scale of cultivation, availability of labor, and economic feasibility. Here are the main types of equipment used in mulberry cultivation:

Land Preparation Equipment

1. Tractors: Tractors of various horsepower are used for ploughing, harrowing, and leveling the land before planting mulberry. Tractors make the land preparation faster and more efficient compared to traditional methods using bullocks or manual labor.

2. Ploughs: Different types of ploughs like disc plough, mouldboard plough, and chisel plough are used for primary tillage to loosen the soil and incorporate crop residues and weeds.

3. Harrows: Harrows like disc harrow and spike tooth harrow are used for secondary tillage to break the clods, level the soil, and prepare a fine tilth for planting.

4. Rotavators: Rotavators are used for preparing the seedbed in a single pass by pulverizing the soil and mixing the crop residues. They are especially useful in heavy soils.

Planting Equipment

1. Mulberry Cutting Machines: Manually operated or power-driven mulberry cutting machines are used to prepare the planting material quickly. These machines can cut 1,400 to 1,500 cuttings per hour, reducing the time and labor required for this operation.

2. Pitting Augers: Tractor-mounted or manually operated pitting augers are used to dig pits of desired size for planting mulberry saplings or cuttings. They make the pitting operation faster and less laborious.

3. Transplanting Tools: Various hand tools like trowels, spades, and dibbers are used for transplanting the mulberry saplings from the nursery to the main field.

Intercultural Equipment

1. Weeders: Different types of weeders are used to control the weeds between the mulberry rows. These include manual weeders like wheel hoe, star weeder, and power weeders like rotary tillers and brush cutters.

2. Pruning Machines: Tractor-mounted or self-propelled pruning machines are used for pruning the mulberry plants after each harvest. These machines can prune one acre of mulberry garden in 2-3 hours, saving time and labor.

3. Sprayers and Dusters: Various types of sprayers and dusters are used for applying pesticides, fungicides, and foliar fertilizers to the mulberry crop. These include

knapsack sprayers, power sprayers, boom sprayers, and tractor-mounted sprayers.

Harvesting Equipment

1. Leaf Harvesters: Tractor-mounted or self-propelled leaf harvesters are used for harvesting mulberry leaves quickly. These machines have a cutting bar that clips the top shoots of the mulberry plants and collects them in a bin or bag.

2. Pruning Shears and Sickles: Hand-operated pruning shears and sickles are used for harvesting individual mulberry leaves or branches selectively. These are used in small-scale mulberry cultivation or for harvesting leaves for young age silkworms.

3. Shoot Harvesters: Knapsack type or tractor-mounted shoot harvesters are used for harvesting mulberry shoots for silkworm rearing. These machines can harvest 1,000-1,200 kg of shoots per hour and are mostly used in medium and large-scale farms.

Post-Harvest Equipment

1. Leaf Choppers: Manual or power-operated leaf choppers are used for chopping the harvested mulberry leaves into small pieces suitable for feeding the silkworms. These machines can chop 225-250 kg of leaves per hour and are most useful for young age silkworm rearing.

2. Leaf Preservation Units: Refrigerated units or cool chambers are used for preserving the excess mulberry leaves

for future use. These units maintain the leaves at a low temperature and high humidity to retain their freshness and nutritive value.

The use of appropriate equipment and machinery in mulberry cultivation can significantly reduce the cost of production, save time and labor, and improve the efficiency of various operations. However, the adoption of mechanization depends on factors like the scale of cultivation, availability of capital, and technical know-how. A judicious combination of manual and mechanical methods is often followed in most mulberry farms for optimal utilization of resources.

Types of equipment used in silkworm rearing

Silkworm rearing involves providing optimal environmental conditions and nutritious food to the silkworms to facilitate their growth and development. Various types of equipment are used at different stages of rearing to ensure proper hygiene, feeding, and cocooning of the silkworms. The major types of equipment used in silkworm rearing are:

Rearing House Equipment

1. Rearing stands or racks: These are the frames used for holding the rearing trays in a vertical arrangement. They are made of wood, bamboo, or iron and have a standard size of 2.5 m height, 1.5 m length, and 0.65-1.0 m width. Each stand can accommodate 10-12 rearing trays.

2. Rearing trays: These are the containers used for keeping the silkworms during rearing. They are made of wood, bamboo, or plastic and come in rectangular or circular shapes. The standard size of a rectangular wooden tray is 3.5' x 2.5', while circular bamboo trays have a diameter of 3.5' to 4'.

3. Ant wells: These are water-filled receptacles placed below the legs of the rearing stand to prevent ants from crawling up and harming the silkworms. They are made of concrete or stone blocks with a groove running around the top to hold water.

4. Feeding basins and leaf baskets: These are used for storing and transporting mulberry leaves for feeding the silkworms. Feeding basins are shallow bamboo baskets, while leaf baskets are larger and deeper.

5. Foam pads and paraffin paper: Foam pads are placed on the rearing trays and covered with paraffin paper to retain moisture and provide a soft bed for the silkworms. The paraffin paper prevents the leaves from drying out and maintains hygiene.

Environmental Control Equipment

1. Hygrometers and thermometers: These instruments are used to monitor the humidity and temperature of the rearing room, which are critical factors for silkworm growth. The ideal temperature range is 24-28°C, and the optimal humidity is 70-85%.

2. Room heaters and air coolers: These are used to maintain the desired temperature and humidity levels in the rearing

room. Room heaters are used during cold weather, while air coolers or wet pads are used during hot and dry conditions.

3. Humidifiers and dehumidifiers: These are used to regulate the humidity levels in the rearing room. Humidifiers add moisture to the air when the humidity is low, while dehumidifiers remove excess moisture when the humidity is high.

4. Ventilation fans and air filters: These are used to ensure proper air circulation and filtration in the rearing room. Ventilation fans help in removing stale air and maintaining oxygen levels, while air filters trap dust and other particles that may harm the silkworms.

Hygiene and Disinfection Equipment

1. Sprayers and dusters: These are used for applying disinfectants, fungicides, and lime powder in the rearing room and on the silkworms. Power sprayers are used for large-scale disinfection, while hand sprayers are used for spot application.

2. Sanitizers and disinfectants: These are chemical compounds used to prevent the growth of disease-causing microbes in the rearing room. Common disinfectants used are bleaching powder, formalin, and chlorine dioxide.

3. Nets and screens: These are used to cover the windows and doors of the rearing room to prevent the entry of pests and predators. Nylon nets and wire mesh screens are commonly used.

4. Hygiene tools: These include brooms, brushes, and dustpans used for cleaning the rearing room and disposing

of silkworm litter and fecal matter. Proper hygiene is essential to prevent disease outbreaks.

Mounting and Harvesting Equipment

1. Mountages: These are the structures on which the mature silkworms spin their cocoons. They are made of bamboo, plastic, or straw and come in different shapes like chandrikes, rotary mountages, or bottle brush mountages.

2. Cocoon harvester: This is a machine used for harvesting the cocoons from the mountages. It has a rotating brush that detaches the cocoons from the mountages and collects them in a container.

3. Cocoon drier: This is used for drying the harvested cocoons to prevent spoilage and maintain quality. It is a chamber with controlled temperature and humidity where the cocoons are dried for 4-5 hours.

In addition to these, other minor equipment like feeding stands, chopsticks, gunny bags, and transportation boxes are also used in silkworm rearing.

The type and quality of equipment used in silkworm rearing have a significant impact on the health and productivity of the silkworms. Modern rearing equipment is designed to provide optimal conditions for silkworm growth while minimizing labor and improving efficiency. Proper maintenance and regular disinfection of the equipment are essential to prevent disease outbreaks and ensure the production of high-quality cocoons.

Innovations in sericulture machinery for improved efficiency

Sericulture, the production of silk through the rearing of silkworms, involves various processes from mulberry cultivation to silk reeling. Traditionally, many of these processes were labour-intensive and relied on manual methods. However, in recent years, there have been significant innovations in sericulture machinery to improve efficiency, productivity, and quality at different stages of silk production.

Mulberry Cultivation Machinery

Mulberry is the sole food plant for the silkworm *Bombyx mori*. Innovations in mulberry cultivation machinery aim to increase leaf yield and quality while reducing labor. Some notable innovations include:

1. Mulberry pruning machines: Motorized pruning machines with reciprocating blades enable quick and uniform pruning of mulberry plants after each harvest. They can prune one acre of mulberry garden in 2-3 hours, saving time and labor compared to manual pruning.

2. Mulberry leaf harvesters: Tractor-mounted or self-propelled leaf harvesters with a cutting bar can efficiently harvest mulberry leaves. They can harvest 1-2 acres per hour, significantly reducing the time and labor required for manual leaf plucking.

3. Solar-powered irrigation systems: Solar-powered drip irrigation systems ensure optimal water supply to mulberry plants while conserving water and energy. They can be automated using sensors and IoT devices for precision irrigation.

Silkworm Rearing Machinery

Innovations in silkworm rearing machinery focus on providing optimal environmental conditions, reducing labor, and improving cocoon quality. Some key innovations are:

1. Automatic silkworm rearing systems: These are multi-tier rearing racks with automated temperature, humidity, and light control. They also have features like automated feeding, bed cleaning, and excreta removal, which significantly reduce labor and improve hygiene.

2. Silkworm egg incubators: Programmable incubators maintain optimal temperature and humidity for uniform hatching of silkworm eggs. They eliminate the need for manual incubation and improve the hatching percentage.

3. Silkworm mountages: Rotary mountages made of plastic or corrugated paper provide more surface area for silkworms to spin cocoons compared to traditional chandrike mountages. They are easier to clean and disinfect, reducing the risk of disease.

Silk Reeling and Processing Machinery

Innovations in silk reeling and processing machinery aim to improve the efficiency, quality, and consistency of silk yarn. Some notable innovations include:

1. Automatic silk reeling machines: These machines integrate the various steps of silk reeling like cocoon cooking, brushing, reeling, and re-reeling. They have features like automatic thread breakage detection, auto-stop, and auto-join, which reduce the need for skilled labor and improve the quality of silk yarn.

2. Multi-end silk reeling machines: These machines can simultaneously reel silk from multiple cocoons (10-20), increasing the reeling efficiency and output. They also have auto-stop and auto-join features to minimize thread breakages.

3. Silk twisting machines: Automatic silk twisting machines twist the silk yarn to improve its strength and evenness. They have precise control over the twist per inch (TPI) and can produce different types of silk threads like crepe, georgette, and chiffon.

4. Cocoon sorting machines: Automated cocoon sorting machines grade the cocoons based on their size, shape, and defects using image processing and machine learning algorithms. They can sort up to 80 cocoons per minute, reducing the time and labor required for manual sorting.

Waste Utilization Machinery

Innovations in waste utilization machinery focus on extracting value from sericulture byproducts like pupae, silk waste, and sericin. Some examples are:

1. Pupae oil extraction machines: These machines extract the oil from silkworm pupae, which is rich in unsaturated fatty acids and has applications in cosmetics, pharmaceuticals, and biodiesel production.

2. Silk waste spinning machines: These machines spin the short fibers from silk waste into yarn, which can be used for making lower-grade silk fabrics, blends, and non-woven products.

3. Sericin extraction machines: These machines extract sericin, a protein present in the silk cocoon, using water or enzymes. Sericin has various biomedical applications like wound healing, skincare, and drug delivery.

Innovations in sericulture machinery have brought about significant improvements in efficiency, productivity, and quality at various stages of silk production. These machines not only reduce the drudgery and labor involved in sericulture but also enable the production of high-quality silk consistently. Adoption of these innovative machines, along with proper training and maintenance, can help sericulture farmers and reelers increase their income and competitiveness. However, the high cost of some of these machines and the need for reliable power supply and technical support remain challenges in their widespread adoption, especially by small-scale sericulture units. Government support through subsidies, credit, and extension services can play a crucial role in promoting the use of innovative sericulture machinery for the sustainable growth of the silk industry.

Maintenance and repair of sericulture equipment

Sericulture involves the use of various equipment and machinery at different stages of silk production, from mulberry cultivation to silk reeling. Proper maintenance and timely repair of this equipment are crucial for ensuring smooth operations, optimizing productivity, and producing high-quality silk. Regular upkeep also extends the lifespan of the machinery, reducing replacement costs.

Maintenance of Mulberry Cultivation Equipment

Mulberry cultivation involves the use of tractors, ploughs, harrows, pruning machines, and sprayers. The key aspects of maintaining this equipment are:

1. Regular cleaning: Remove dirt, debris, and plant residues from the equipment after each use. This prevents corrosion and ensures proper functioning of moving parts.

2. Lubrication: Regularly grease and oil the moving parts like gears, bearings, and chains as per the manufacturer's guidelines. This reduces friction and wear.

3. Sharpening and adjustment: Keep the cutting blades of pruning machines and ploughs sharp and properly adjusted for efficient operation. Dull or misaligned blades can damage the plants and reduce productivity.

4. Proper storage: Store the equipment in a dry and covered place to protect them from rain, dust, and pests. Apply rust-preventive coatings on exposed metal parts.

5. Periodic inspection: Regularly inspect the equipment for any signs of wear, damage, or malfunctioning. Replace worn-out parts and repair damages promptly.

Maintenance of Silkworm Rearing Equipment

Silkworm rearing involves the use of rearing trays, stands, mountages, and environmental control devices. The key aspects of maintaining this equipment are:

1. Disinfection: Thoroughly clean and disinfect the rearing trays, stands, and mountages before and after each rearing cycle. Use recommended disinfectants like bleaching powder, chlorine dioxide, or formalin to prevent disease outbreaks.

2. Repair and replacement: Check the rearing trays and stands for any cracks, holes, or broken parts. Repair or replace damaged equipment to prevent contamination and ensure stability.

3. Calibration: Regularly calibrate the temperature and humidity control devices to ensure they provide accurate readings and maintain optimal rearing conditions.

4. Filter cleaning: Clean or replace the filters of air circulators and ventilators periodically to maintain air quality and prevent the entry of pathogens.

5. Proper storage: Store the rearing equipment in a clean, dry, and pest-free place during the off-season. Protect them from rodents and insects that may harbor pathogens.

Maintenance of Silk Reeling Equipment

Silk reeling involves the use of reeling basins, cocoon boiling units, reeling machines, and twisting machines. The key aspects of maintaining this equipment are:

1. Regular cleaning: Clean the reeling basins, cocoon boiling units, and reeling machines after each use to remove silk waste, sericin deposits, and other residues. This prevents contamination and ensures the quality of the silk.

2. Lubrication: Regularly lubricate the moving parts of reeling and twisting machines, such as gears, bearings, and spindles, to reduce friction and wear. Use recommended grade oils and greases.

3. Tension adjustment: Periodically check and adjust the tension of the reeling and twisting mechanisms to ensure consistent thickness and quality of the silk filaments.

4. Replacement of worn-out parts: Regularly inspect the reeling and twisting machines for worn-out or damaged parts like croissure pulleys, distributor gears, and traverse mechanisms. Replace them promptly to avoid breakages and maintain the quality of the silk.

5. Proper storage: Store the reeling and twisting machines in a clean, dry, and dust-free environment during the off-season. Cover them with plastic sheets to protect from moisture and pests.

Repair of Sericulture Equipment

Despite regular maintenance, sericulture equipment may occasionally break down or malfunction due to wear and tear, overuse, or accidents. In such cases, timely repair is essential to minimize downtime and losses. The key aspects of repairing sericulture equipment are:

1. Troubleshooting: Identify the cause of the breakdown or malfunction through careful observation and testing. Consult the equipment manual or experienced technicians for guidance.

2. Spare parts inventory: Maintain an inventory of commonly required spare parts like gears, bearings, belts, and electronic components. This reduces the time required for repairs.

3. Skilled technicians: Employ or contract skilled technicians who are familiar with the functioning and repair of sericulture equipment. Provide them with necessary tools and training.

4. Timely repair: Carry out repairs promptly to minimize the impact on production schedules. Have backup equipment or alternative arrangements to avoid complete stoppage of work.

5. Testing and calibration: After the repair, test the equipment thoroughly to ensure it is functioning properly and safely. Calibrate the equipment if required to maintain accuracy and consistency.

Regular maintenance and timely repair of sericulture equipment are essential for the smooth functioning and productivity of the silk industry. Sericulture farmers and reelers should develop and follow a maintenance schedule, train their workers on proper equipment handling, and keep records of maintenance and repair activities. Seeking the guidance of equipment manufacturers, sericulture experts, and skilled technicians can help in optimizing the performance and lifespan of the equipment. Investing in maintenance and repair not only reduces breakdowns and production losses but also ensures the quality and competitiveness of the silk produced.

Chapter 12

Sericulture and Rural Development

Role of sericulture in poverty alleviation and rural employment generation

Sericulture, the production of silk through rearing of silkworms, plays a vital role in alleviating poverty and generating employment opportunities in rural areas. Being an agro-based and labour-intensive industry, sericulture provides a viable and sustainable livelihood option for the rural poor, especially women and marginalized communities. The various aspects of sericulture's contribution to poverty reduction and rural employment are discussed below:

Employment Generation

Sericulture involves a series of activities from mulberry cultivation to silk fabric production, each creating employment at different stages:

1. Mulberry cultivation: Planting, pruning, fertilizing, irrigating, and harvesting mulberry leaves provides employment to farmers and agricultural laborers.

2. Silkworm rearing: Raising silkworms from eggs to cocoons engages rural households, particularly women, in silkworm brushing, feeding, bed cleaning, and disinfection.

3. Cocoon harvesting and marketing: Harvesting, sorting, and transporting cocoons to markets creates jobs for rural youth and women.

4. Silk reeling and twisting: The process of unwinding silk filaments from cocoons and twisting them into yarn employs skilled and semi-skilled workers in reeling units and twisting factories.

5. Silk weaving and fabric production: Weaving silk yarn into fabrics and producing finished silk products engages handloom weavers, designers, and artisans.

It is estimated that sericulture can generate employment of 11 person-days per kg of raw silk production. One hectare of mulberry plantation can provide year-round employment to about 12-13 people. In India, sericulture is practiced in about 52,360 villages, providing livelihood to around 9.47 lakh families and engaging over 7.56 million people, mostly small and marginal farmers, women, and rural artisans.

Income Generation

Sericulture provides a steady source of income to rural families as it can be practiced 4-6 times a year, unlike most agricultural crops which provide income only once or twice a year. The income from sericulture is estimated to be 5-6 times higher than that from agricultural crops.

Studies have shown that most sericulture farmers in India earn Rs. 5000 to Rs. 15000 per annum from cocoon production. Silk reeling and weaving activities further enhance the income of rural artisans. The high value of silk and its global demand ensure remunerative prices for the producers.

Women Empowerment

Sericulture is a women-friendly occupation as most of its activities are home-based and can be done alongside household chores. About 60% of the labor force in sericulture is constituted by women. Silkworm rearing is particularly suitable for women as it requires patience, care, and attention to detail.

Engaging in sericulture gives women an opportunity to earn an independent income, contribute to household finances, and enhance their decision-making power. It boosts their self-confidence and social status in the community. Studies have shown that women's participation in sericulture has led to better child education, health, and nutrition outcomes.

Low Capital Investment

Sericulture requires low capital investment compared to other industries, making it suitable for rural entrepreneurs. The tools and equipment needed for silkworm rearing and reeling are simple and affordable. Government schemes and institutional credit further facilitate the adoption of sericulture by providing subsidies, training, and marketing support.

Eco-friendly and Sustainable

Sericulture is an eco-friendly activity as it involves no use of chemical fertilizers or pesticides in mulberry cultivation. The waste from silkworm rearing, such as litter and pupae, can be used as organic manure and animal feed. Mulberry plants help in soil conservation, carbon sequestration, and biodiversity preservation. Thus, sericulture contributes to sustainable rural development.

Prevents Rural-Urban Migration

Sericulture, being a rural-based industry, provides employment and income opportunities to the rural poor in their own villages. This helps in reducing the migration of rural youth to urban areas in search of jobs, thus preventing the growth of urban slums and associated social problems. Sericulture enables rural people to lead a dignified life in their own communities.

Sericulture plays a crucial role in poverty alleviation and rural employment generation by providing a sustainable and remunerative livelihood option to the rural poor. It empowers women, promotes eco-friendly practices, and prevents rural-urban migration. With increasing global demand for silk and supportive government policies, sericulture has the potential to transform the rural economy and contribute to inclusive growth. However, challenges such as climate change, price fluctuations, and inadequate infrastructure need to be addressed through research, extension, and policy support to realize the full potential of sericulture in poverty reduction and rural development.

Sericulture-based rural industries and entrepreneurship development

Sericulture is an important agro-based cottage industry that plays a vital role in the socio-economic development of rural areas. It involves the cultivation of mulberry plants, rearing of silkworms, production of cocoons, reeling of silk yarn, and weaving of silk fabrics. Sericulture provides ample opportunities for entrepreneurship development and establishment of rural industries due to its low capital investment, high employment potential, and eco-friendly nature.

Sericulture as a Rural Industry

Sericulture is highly suited for rural areas because of the following reasons:

1. Agro-based: Sericulture is an agricultural activity that involves the cultivation of mulberry plants and rearing of silkworms. It can be easily integrated with other farming activities and provides additional income to farmers.

2. Labor-intensive: Sericulture involves various manual operations like leaf plucking, silkworm rearing, cocoon harvesting, and silk reeling. It generates employment for both skilled and unskilled workers, especially women, in rural areas.

3. Low capital investment: Sericulture does not require heavy machinery or infrastructure. It can be started with minimal investment in mulberry plantation, rearing sheds, and basic equipment.

4. Short gestation period: Unlike other tree crops, mulberry starts yielding leaves within six months of planting. Silkworms have a short life cycle of 25-30 days, enabling multiple crops per year and quick returns.

5. Eco-friendly: Sericulture is an environment-friendly activity as it involves no use of chemical fertilizers or pesticides. Mulberry plants help in soil conservation and the waste from silkworm rearing can be used as organic manure.

Entrepreneurship Opportunities in Sericulture

Sericulture offers various entrepreneurship opportunities for rural youth and women:

1. Mulberry cultivation: Entrepreneurs can take up mulberry cultivation on a commercial scale to supply leaves to silkworm rearers. High-yielding mulberry varieties and improved package of practices can enhance leaf yield and quality.

2. Silkworm seed production: Entrepreneurs can establish silkworm seed production units to supply disease-free layings (eggs) to rearers. Strict hygiene, quality control, and timely supply are crucial for this venture.

3. Silkworm rearing: Rearing silkworms to produce cocoons is the core activity of sericulture. Entrepreneurs can set up rearing sheds with modern equipment and adopt scientific methods to increase cocoon yield and quality.

4. Cocoon marketing: Entrepreneurs can act as cocoon traders by procuring cocoons from rearers and supplying them to reeling units. Proper grading, storage, and transportation of cocoons are important for this business.

5. Silk reeling: Reeling is the process of unwinding silk filaments from cocoons to produce raw silk yarn. Entrepreneurs can establish automatic or semi-automatic reeling units to produce high-quality silk.

6. Silk weaving: Weaving is the process of making silk fabrics from yarn. Entrepreneurs can set up handloom or power loom units to produce traditional or innovative silk products like sarees, dress materials, stoles, etc.

7. Silk processing: Entrepreneurs can venture into silk dyeing, printing, finishing, and other value-addition processes to cater to the changing market demands.

8. Waste utilization: Silkworm pupae, silk waste, and other byproducts of sericulture can be used to make various products like pupae oil, silk protein, sericin, etc. Entrepreneurs can explore these avenues for additional income.

Government Support for Sericulture Entrepreneurship

The central and state governments in India provide various schemes and incentives to promote sericulture entrepreneurship:

1. Subsidies: Financial assistance is provided for mulberry plantation, construction of rearing sheds, purchase of equipment, establishment of reeling and weaving units, etc.

2. Training: Entrepreneurship development programs, skill upgradation trainings, and exposure visits are organized by sericulture departments and research institutes.

3. Infrastructure: Common facility centers for reeling, weaving, and processing are established in sericulture clusters to provide access to modern machinery and technical guidance.

4. Marketing: Silk expos, fairs, and e-commerce platforms are promoted to provide market linkages for sericulture entrepreneurs.

5. Credit: Loans at concessional rates are provided by banks and financial institutions for sericulture activities under priority sector lending.

Sericulture is a promising sector for entrepreneurship development in rural areas. It has the potential to generate employment, increase incomes, and promote sustainable rural industrialization. With the growing demand for silk and supportive government policies, sericulture can attract more entrepreneurs and transform the rural economy. However, challenges like price fluctuations, quality control, and market linkages need to be addressed through research, extension, and institutional support to realize the full potential of sericulture entrepreneurship.

Government schemes and incentives for promotion of sericulture

The central and state governments in India have introduced several schemes and incentives to promote sericulture as a viable livelihood option for rural communities. These initiatives aim to increase silk production, improve the quality of silk, and enhance the income of sericulture farmers and other stakeholders in the silk value chain.

Central Silk Board (CSB) Schemes

The Central Silk Board, under the Ministry of Textiles, Government of India, is the apex body for the development of the silk industry in the country. Some of the key schemes implemented by CSB are:

1. Catalytic Development Programme (CDP): This is a flagship scheme of CSB that provides financial assistance to sericulture projects in a project mode, focusing on cluster development. The scheme supports various components like mulberry plantation, silkworm seed production, cocoon production, silk reeling, and post-cocoon processes. The funding pattern is 65% by CSB, 25% by the state government, and 10% by the beneficiary.

2. Silk Samagra: This is an integrated scheme for the development of silk industry, covering the entire silk value chain from host plant cultivation to silk product development. The scheme has four components - Research & Development, Seed Organizations, Coordination & Market Development, and Quality Certification Systems. It provides support for the production of high-quality silkworm seeds, improved silk reeling machines, and capacity building of sericulture stakeholders.

3. Cluster Promotion Programme: This scheme aims to establish sericulture clusters in identified potential areas, with a focus on the participation of women and scheduled caste/tribe beneficiaries. Each cluster covers 500-1000 hectares of mulberry plantation and supports 1000-2000 beneficiaries. The scheme provides financial assistance for the development of common infrastructure like irrigation, rearing sheds, and post-cocoon facilities.

State Government Schemes

Various state governments in India have also introduced their own schemes and incentives to promote sericulture, tailored to the specific needs and potential of the state. Some examples are:

1. Karnataka Sericulture Development Schemes: Karnataka, the leading silk producing state in India, has several schemes for the development of sericulture. These include subsidies for the construction of rearing sheds, irrigation facilities, and purchase of improved reeling machines. The state also provides training and extension services to sericulture farmers through its network of Technical Service Centres.

2. Andhra Pradesh Sericulture Schemes: The Government of Andhra Pradesh provides subsidies for the establishment of mulberry gardens, construction of rearing sheds, and purchase of shoot rearing equipment. The state also offers incentives for the production of bivoltine silk, which fetches higher prices in the market.

3. Tamil Nadu Sericulture Schemes: The Tamil Nadu government provides subsidies for the establishment of mulberry gardens, drip irrigation, and construction of rearing sheds. The state also has a scheme for the promotion of organic sericulture, which provides additional incentives for farmers adopting organic practices.

4. West Bengal Sericulture Schemes: The Government of West Bengal provides financial assistance for the establishment of mulberry gardens, construction of rearing houses, and purchase of rearing equipment. The state also has a scheme for the promotion of tasar sericulture in tribal areas, which provides subsidies for host plant cultivation and rearing infrastructure.

Incentives for Silk Reeling and Weaving

In addition to schemes for sericulture farmers, the government also provides incentives for the development of silk reeling and weaving sectors:

1. Silk Reeling Scheme: The CSB provides financial assistance for the establishment of automatic and semi-automatic silk reeling units. The scheme covers 50% of the cost of machinery, subject to a maximum of Rs. 50 lakh per unit. The beneficiary has to contribute 25% of the cost, while the remaining 25% can be financed through bank loans.

2. Silk Weaving Scheme: The government provides subsidies for the modernization of silk handlooms and powerlooms. The scheme covers 50% of the cost of upgradation, subject to a maximum of Rs. 20,000 per handloom and Rs. 1 lakh per powerloom. Weavers' cooperatives and self-help groups are eligible for higher subsidies.

3. Silk Mark Scheme: To ensure the purity and quality of silk, the government has introduced the Silk Mark scheme. Silk products bearing the Silk Mark label are guaranteed to be made of pure and natural silk. The scheme provides incentives for silk traders and retailers to adopt the Silk Mark certification.

Other Incentives and Support Measures

Apart from the specific schemes mentioned above, the government also provides various other incentives and support measures for the promotion of sericulture:

1. Subsidies for the purchase of silkworm eggs, disinfectants, and other inputs

2. Exemption of excise duty on raw silk and silk yarn

3. Concessional rates of interest on loans for sericulture activities

4. Support for the development of infrastructure like cocoon markets, silk exchanges, and testing laboratories

5. Capacity building and training programs for sericulture farmers, reelers, and weavers

6. Promotion of sericulture-based tourism and handicrafts

The government of India recognizes the potential of sericulture in generating employment, alleviating poverty, and promoting inclusive growth in rural areas. The various schemes and incentives provided by the central and state governments have played a crucial role in the development of the sericulture industry in the country. However, there is still scope for further strengthening of these initiatives, particularly in terms of increasing the coverage of beneficiaries, improving the quality and productivity of silk, and promoting value addition and market linkages. A collaborative effort between the government, industry, and other stakeholders is necessary to realize the full potential of sericulture in India.

Chapter 13

Sericulture and Women Empowerment

Participation of women in sericulture activities

Sericulture, the production of silk through rearing of silkworms, is a highly labour-intensive agro-based cottage industry that provides ample opportunities for the involvement of women. In fact, women's participation is crucial in almost all the activities of sericulture, from mulberry cultivation to silk fabric production. It is estimated that women constitute about 60% of the total workforce engaged in sericulture in India.

Mulberry Cultivation

Mulberry is the sole food plant for the silkworm *Bombyx mori*. Women actively participate in various activities related to mulberry cultivation such as:

- Planting and maintenance of mulberry saplings

- Weeding and inter-cultivation operations

- Application of manures and fertilizers

- Irrigation and pruning of mulberry plants

- Harvesting and transportation of mulberry leaves

Studies have shown that women's participation in mulberry cultivation ranges from 60-90% depending on the specific activity and region.

Silkworm Rearing

Silkworm rearing involves providing the right environmental conditions and nutritious mulberry leaves to the silkworms for their growth and development. Women play a dominant role in this activity as it requires patience, care, and attention to detail. The key activities performed by women in silkworm rearing are:

- Incubation and hatching of silkworm eggs

- Brushing (feeding) of young silkworms

- Bed cleaning and disinfection

- Spacing of grown-up silkworms

- Mounting of mature silkworms for cocoon spinning

- Harvesting and sorting of cocoons

It is estimated that women contribute about 60-70% of the total labour in silkworm rearing. The indoor nature of this activity and its compatibility with household chores make it highly suitable for women's participation.

Silk Reeling and Spinning

Silk reeling involves unwinding the silk filament from the cocoons and combining them into a yarn. Women's nimble fingers and patience make them highly suitable for this delicate task. In the traditional charkha reeling, women constitute the majority of the workforce. Even in the modern filatures, women are employed in large numbers for tasks like cocoon sorting, cooking, and silk waste spinning.

Silk Weaving and Fabric Production

Women's participation in silk weaving varies across regions and type of fabrics. In the traditional handloom sector, women are involved in various pre-loom and post-loom activities such as:

- Bobbin winding and pirn winding

- Joining of warp threads and drawing of designs

- Assisting in the weaving process

- Dyeing and printing of silk fabrics

- Embroidery and other value-addition activities

In the modern power loom sector, women are employed in activities like design making, quality checking, and packaging.

Factors Enabling Women's Participation

Several factors make sericulture a highly suitable occupation for women:

1. Indoor and home-based nature of most activities

2. Compatibility with household chores and family responsibilities

3. Requirement of patience, care, and dexterity rather than physical strength

4. Frequent and continuous income generation throughout the year

5. Potential for self-employment and entrepreneurship development

Challenges and Way Forward

Despite the high participation of women in sericulture, their contributions often remain invisible and undervalued. Women face several challenges such as:

- Lack of ownership and control over productive resources like land, credit, and technology

- Limited access to training, extension services, and market information

- Wage disparities and discrimination in employment opportunities

- Double burden of productive and reproductive responsibilities

-Limited role in decision-making and leadership positions

To enhance women's participation and empowerment in sericulture, there is a need for:

- Gender-sensitive policies and programs that recognize and support women's contributions

- Improved access to credit, technology, and extension services for women

- Capacity building and skill upgradation through training and exposure visits

- Promotion of women-friendly tools and technologies to reduce drudgery

- Collectivization and organization of women into self-help groups and cooperatives

- Sensitization of men and community leaders about gender equality and women's rights

Women's participation is the backbone of the sericulture industry. Recognizing and supporting women's contributions is crucial for the sustainable development of sericulture and the empowerment of rural women. A multi-pronged approach involving policy support, technological interventions, and social mobilization is needed to tap the full potential of women in sericulture.

Sericulture as a tool for women empowerment and gender equality

Sericulture, the production of silk through the rearing of silkworms, is an agro-based cottage industry that has immense potential for promoting women empowerment and gender equality in rural areas. Women's participation is integral to all stages of sericulture, from mulberry cultivation to silk fabric production. Engaging in sericulture activities not only provides women with a source of income but also enhances their decision-making power, social status, and overall well-being.

Economic Empowerment

Sericulture provides a viable and sustainable livelihood option for rural women, especially those from small and marginal farming households. The low capital investment, short gestation period, and indoor nature of most activities make sericulture highly suitable for women's participation. Studies have shown that women engaged in sericulture earn a significant portion of their household income, ranging from 30-60% depending on the region and type of activity.

The income earned from sericulture enables women to contribute to household expenses, invest in their children's education and health, and create assets in their own name. This financial independence enhances women's bargaining power within the household and gives them greater control over their lives.

Social Empowerment

Participation in sericulture activities also leads to the social empowerment of women. The collective nature of many sericulture operations, such as silkworm rearing and silk reeling, provides women with opportunities to interact with their peers, share knowledge and skills, and build social networks. This social capital helps women to overcome their isolation, gain confidence, and assert their rights.

Sericulture-based self-help groups (SHGs) and cooperatives have emerged as effective platforms for women's empowerment. These organizations not only provide women with access to credit, technology, and markets but also foster leadership skills, collective action, and political participation. Women's SHGs have successfully challenged social norms, addressed issues like domestic violence and child marriage, and promoted gender equality in their communities.

Decision-Making Power

Engaging in sericulture gives women a greater say in household decision-making. As women contribute significantly to household income, they gain more respect and authority within the family. Studies have shown that women engaged in sericulture have a higher level of autonomy in decisions related to their own health, children's education, and household purchases compared to non-sericulture households.

At the community level, women's participation in sericulture-based organizations like SHGs and cooperatives enables them to influence decisions related to the development and governance of their villages. Women leaders from these organizations have successfully contested local body elections and raised their voice against social injustices.

Access to Resources and Services

Sericulture programs and policies that specifically target women have helped to improve their access to productive resources and services. For example, the Mahila Kisan Sashaktikaran Pariyojana (MKSP) in India, which aims to empower women farmers, has provided sericulture training, inputs, and marketing support to women's collectives. Such initiatives have helped women to overcome barriers like lack of land ownership, limited access to credit and technology, and gender-based discrimination in extension services.

Challenges and Way Forward

Despite the potential of sericulture for women's empowerment, several challenges persist. Women often face a double burden of productive and reproductive responsibilities, which limits their ability to fully engage in sericulture activities. The lack of ownership and control over productive resources like land, credit, and technology also constrains women's participation and benefits from sericulture.

Moreover, the gender division of labour in sericulture often relegates women to low-paid and labour-intensive tasks like silkworm rearing and silk reeling, while men dominate the more profitable activities like cocoon trading and silk weaving. Gender wage gaps and occupational segregation in sericulture need to be addressed through policies and programs that promote equal opportunities and fair remuneration for women.

To fully harness the potential of sericulture for women's empowerment, there is a need for:

- Gender-responsive policies and programs that recognize and support women's contributions to sericulture

- Improved access to land, credit, technology, and extension services for women sericulture farmers and entrepreneurs

- Capacity building and skill upgradation of women through training, exposure visits, and mentoring

- Promotion of women-friendly tools and technologies to reduce drudgery and occupational health hazards

- Strengthening of women's collectives like SHGs and cooperatives for collective action and bargaining power

- Sensitization of men and community leaders about gender equality and women's rights

- Addressing social norms and practices that discriminate against women and limit their mobility and decision-making power

Sericulture has the potential to be a powerful tool for women's empowerment and gender equality in rural areas. By providing women with a sustainable livelihood, social capital, and decision-making power, sericulture can help to challenge gender stereotypes, reduce poverty, and promote inclusive development. However, realizing this potential requires a concerted effort from policymakers, development practitioners, and communities to create an enabling environment for women's participation and leadership in sericulture. With the right policies, investments, and social change, sericulture can become a catalyst for women's empowerment and gender equality in the rural landscape.

Success stories of women entrepreneurs in sericulture

Sericulture, being a highly labour-intensive and home-based activity, provides ample opportunities for women to engage as entrepreneurs. Many women have overcome challenges and made significant contributions to the sericulture industry through their entrepreneurial ventures. Here are a few notable success stories:

Padmini Bhise, India

Padmini Bhise, a woman from Maharashtra, India, transformed her life by taking up sericulture entrepreneurship. Starting with just a small patch of land for mulberry cultivation and a few silkworms, she gradually expanded her sericulture activities and became successful in silk production. Her success story has motivated many other women in her village to take up sericulture as a livelihood option.

Ishikawa Yoshie, Japan

Known as the "Silk Queen" of Japan, Ishikawa Yoshie is a pioneering woman entrepreneur in the sericulture sector. She introduced innovative techniques in silkworm rearing to enhance silk productivity. Her initiatives not only boosted the domestic silk industry but also contributed to Japan's silk exports.

Nila Madhaba Patra, India

Nila Madhaba Patra, hailing from Odisha, India, is a successful woman entrepreneur in the sericulture sector. Along with her husband, she runs a silk farm where they have trained many women in sericulture skills. Their efforts have helped other women in their community gain financial independence through silk production.

Mei Zhan, China

Mei Zhan, a farmer from Zhejiang Province, China, transformed her life through sericulture entrepreneurship. After learning modern sericulture techniques, she established a thriving silk farm. Mei Zhan's success story exemplifies how sericulture is helping rural women in China improve their standard of living and achieve self-reliance.

Sandhya Rani Mahala, India

Sandhya Rani Mahala from Jajpur, Odisha, India, is a successful mushroom and sericulture entrepreneur. Starting with a small scale, she expanded her enterprise and now cultivates nearly 5000 mushroom beds annually, earning a net profit of over Rs. 2 lakhs. She has motivated and trained many women SHGs in her area to take up mushroom and sericulture entrepreneurship.

Lalhluni, India

Lalhluni, a tribal woman from Mizoram, India, is a leading sericulture farmer and entrepreneur. Apart from earning substantially from silkworm rearing and cocoon production, she also cultivates inter-crops like banana, pineapple, and orange in her mulberry garden, which provides additional income. Her integrated farming approach has made her a role model for other tribal women in Mizoram.

These success stories demonstrate the grit, innovation, and entrepreneurial spirit of women sericulturists. They have not only improved their own lives but have also inspired and empowered other women in their communities to take up sericulture. These women have made significant contributions to their local economies and to the sericulture industry as a whole.

Women's active participation in all stages of the silk production process, from traditional sericulture practices to modern entrepreneurship, is crucial for the success and sustainability of the industry. Sericulture provides women with opportunities for social and economic empowerment, making it an effective tool for women's livelihoods and gender equality in many communities. With the right skills, resources, and an enabling environment, more women can emerge as successful sericulture entrepreneurs, contributing to their own development as well as the growth of the silk sector.

Chapter 14

Sericulture Waste Utilization

Types of waste generated in sericulture and their disposal

Sericulture, the production of silk through rearing of silkworms, involves various activities such as mulberry cultivation, silkworm rearing, silk reeling, and fabric production. Each of these stages generates different types of waste that need to be managed effectively to prevent environmental pollution and health hazards. The major types of waste generated in sericulture are:

Mulberry Cultivation Waste

Mulberry is the sole food plant for the silkworm *Bombyx mori*. Mulberry cultivation generates the following types of waste:

1. Pruning waste: Mulberry plants are pruned regularly to encourage new leaf growth. The pruned branches, twigs, and leaves constitute the pruning waste.

2. Leaf litter: Fallen mulberry leaves, which are not consumed by the silkworms, accumulate as leaf litter.

3. Weed biomass: Weeds growing in the mulberry fields are removed periodically and form the weed waste.

Disposal methods:

- Pruning waste and leaf litter can be composted to produce organic manure for the mulberry plants.

- Weed biomass can be used as fodder for cattle or composted.

- Mulberry twigs and branches can be used as fuel for cooking or heating.

Silkworm Rearing Waste

Silkworm rearing involves feeding the worms with mulberry leaves and facilitating their growth and cocoon production. The following wastes are generated during this process:

1. Silkworm litter: The excreta of silkworms, along with the unconsumed mulberry leaves and other debris, constitute the silkworm litter. It is the major waste generated during rearing, amounting to about 20-30 kg per 100 dfls (disease free layings).

2. Diseased and dead larvae: Silkworms affected by diseases like grasserie, flacherie, muscardine, etc. die during the rearing process. Dead worms, if not removed promptly, can spread the infection to healthy worms.

3. Cocoon waste: Unsuitable cocoons, such as stained, malformed, or pierced ones, are rejected during the sorting process and form the cocoon waste.

Disposal methods:

- Silkworm litter can be composted or vermicomposted to produce nutrient-rich manure for mulberry plants. Composting helps in killing the pathogens and converting the waste into a stable, odorless product.

- Diseased and dead larvae should be incinerated or buried deep in the soil away from the rearing area to prevent the spread of diseases.

- Unsuitable cocoons can be used for extracting silk fibers through the spun silk process. The pupae from these cocoons can be used as poultry or fish feed after oil extraction.

Silk Reeling Waste

Silk reeling is the process of unwinding the silk filaments from the cocoons and combining them into a yarn. The following wastes are generated during reeling:

1. Reeling waste: It includes the silk filaments that break during the reeling process, cocoons that are not completely reelable, and the outer and inner layers of the cocoon that are too coarse or fine for reeling.

2. Pupae: The silkworm pupae, after the silk is reeled from the cocoons, are a major byproduct of the reeling industry.

3. Wastewater: Silk reeling generates wastewater containing sericin, the gummy protein coating of the silk fibers, and other impurities.

Disposal methods:

- Reeling waste can be processed into spun silk, which has various textile applications.

- Silkworm pupae are rich in protein and oil. After oil extraction, the pupae can be used as animal feed or fertilizer. The pupal oil has applications in cosmetics and pharmaceuticals.

- Silk reeling wastewater should be treated before disposal to remove the organic load and comply with the effluent discharge standards. The wastewater can be treated using physical, chemical, and biological methods such as screening, settling, coagulation, and activated sludge process.

Other Wastes

Apart from the above major wastes, sericulture also generates some other wastes like:

- Plastic waste from rearing trays, mountages, and packaging materials

- Waste cocoons from seed production and grainage operations

- Waste silk from weaving and fabric production

These wastes should be collected separately and recycled or disposed of as per the local waste management regulations.

Effective management of sericulture waste is crucial for the sustainability of the silk industry. Proper waste disposal methods not only prevent environmental pollution but also provide opportunities for generating value-added products like organic manure, spun silk, and pupal oil. Sericulture waste management should adopt the principles of reduce, reuse, and recycle to minimize the waste generation and maximize the resource recovery. Awareness among the sericulture farmers and industry stakeholders about the importance of waste management and the available technologies for waste utilization is essential for the eco-friendly and sustainable growth of the sericulture sector.

Value addition and utilization of sericulture wastes

Sericulture, the production of silk through rearing of silkworms, generates substantial quantities of waste at various stages. The major wastes include silkworm litter, pupal waste, silk reeling waste, and mulberry cultivation waste. Proper utilization of these wastes not only prevents environmental pollution but also provides additional income to sericulture farmers. Value addition to sericulture wastes involves converting them into useful products of higher economic value. The following are some of the important ways of value addition and utilization of sericulture wastes:

Vermicomposting

Silkworm litter, which consists of silkworm excreta, unconsumed mulberry leaves, and other debris, is a rich source of organic matter and nutrients. It can be effectively converted into nutrient-rich vermicompost by using earthworms like Eisenia fetida and Eudrilus eugeniae. The process involves mixing the silkworm litter with cow dung and allowing the earthworms to feed on it for 45-60 days. The resulting vermicompost is an excellent organic fertilizer for crops, including mulberry. Studies have shown that application of vermicompost made from sericulture waste improves soil fertility, mulberry leaf yield, and cocoon production.

Mushroom Cultivation

Spent silkworm pupae and mulberry cultivation waste like pruned branches and leaves can be used as substrates for mushroom cultivation. Oyster mushroom (Pleurotus spp.) and milky mushroom (Calocybe indica) grow well on these substrates after proper treatment and sterilization. Mushroom cultivation on sericulture wastes provides an additional source of income and nutrition to sericulture farmers. The spent mushroom substrate can further be used as organic manure for crops.

Biogas Production

Silkworm pupal waste and litter can be used as feedstock for biogas production through anaerobic digestion. The biogas, which is a mixture of methane and carbon dioxide, can be used as a renewable fuel for cooking and lighting. The digested slurry is a good organic fertilizer rich in nitrogen, phosphorus, and potassium. Biogas production from sericulture wastes not only generates clean energy but also helps in waste management.

Silkworm Pupal Oil and Meal

Silkworm pupae, which are a byproduct of silk reeling, contain about 30-40% oil and 50-60% protein on dry weight basis. The oil can be extracted by solvent extraction or expeller pressing and refined for various uses. Silkworm pupal oil is rich in unsaturated fatty acids like oleic and linoleic acids and has applications in food, cosmetics, and biodiesel production. The defatted pupal meal is a high-protein feed ingredient for poultry, fish, and livestock. It can replace fishmeal in animal diets and reduce the cost of production.

Sericin Extraction

Sericin is a gummy protein that constitutes about 25-30% of the silk cocoon. It is removed during the silk reeling process and is a major component of silk reeling waste water. Sericin can be extracted from the waste water by membrane filtration, acid precipitation, or enzymatic hydrolysis. Sericin has various biomedical applications due to its moisturizing, antioxidant, and wound healing properties. It is used in cosmetics, pharmaceuticals, and functional foods. Extraction of sericin from reeling waste adds value to the byproduct and reduces the pollution load of the effluent.

Handicrafts and Decorative Items

Silk reeling waste like pierced cocoons, flimsy cocoons, and silk fiber waste can be used for making handicrafts and decorative items. These include silk flowers, greeting cards, wall hangings, lampshades, and jewelry. The cocoons can be dyed in various colors and used for making garlands, bouquets, and other ornamental products. Such value-added products fetch higher prices than the raw silk waste and provide employment opportunities for rural artisans.

Biocomposites and Packaging Materials

Mulberry stalks and branches, which are pruned periodically, are a lignocellulosic biomass that can be used for making biocomposites and packaging materials. The biomass can be chipped, pulped, and molded into biodegradable plates, cups, and containers. It can also be used as a filler in polymer composites to improve their mechanical and thermal properties. Such eco-friendly products have a growing demand due to increasing environmental concerns and regulations on plastic use.

Sericulture wastes are a valuable biomass that can be converted into various value-added products through appropriate technologies. Vermicomposting, mushroom cultivation, biogas production, silkworm pupal oil extraction, sericin recovery, handicrafts making, and biocomposite production are some of the promising ways of utilizing sericulture wastes. These not only generate additional income for sericulture farmers but also contribute to waste management and environmental sustainability. Research and development efforts are needed to optimize the processes, improve the product quality, and expand the market for such value-added products from sericulture wastes. Policy support and entrepreneurship development are also essential to promote the adoption of these technologies by sericulture farmers and rural communities.

Vermicomposting and biogas production from sericulture waste

Sericulture, the rearing of silkworms for silk production, generates substantial quantities of organic waste at various stages. The major wastes include silkworm litter (excreta, unconsumed mulberry leaves, and other debris), silkworm pupae, and mulberry cultivation waste (pruning waste, leaf litter, etc.). Proper management and value addition of these wastes through vermicomposting and biogas production can provide additional income to sericulture farmers while ensuring environmental sustainability.

Vermicomposting of Sericulture Waste

Vermicomposting is an eco-friendly and efficient method of converting sericulture waste into nutrient-rich organic manure using earthworms. The process involves the following steps:

1. Waste collection and pre-processing: Silkworm litter and other sericulture wastes are collected and chopped or shredded to smaller pieces for faster decomposition.

2. Mixing with cow dung: The pre-processed waste is mixed with cow dung in a ratio of 3:1 to provide the right carbon-nitrogen balance and inoculum for the earthworms.

3. Preparation of vermibed: A vermibed of suitable size (e.g., 2.4 x 0.6 x 0.6 m) is prepared with a layer of bedding material like coir pith or shredded paper, followed by the waste-cow dung mixture.

4. Introduction of earthworms: Epigeic earthworm species like Eisenia fetida or Eudrilus eugeniae are introduced into the vermibed at a density of 1-2 kg worms per m².

5. Maintenance of optimal conditions: The vermibed is maintained at 25-30°C temperature, 60-80% moisture content, and 7.0-7.5 pH for optimal worm activity and decomposition.

6. Harvesting of vermicompost: After 45-60 days, the vermicompost is harvested, sieved, and stored for application to crops. A well-maintained vermibed can yield 2.5-3.0 tons of vermicompost per year.

Vermicompost produced from sericulture waste is rich in nutrients like nitrogen, phosphorus, potassium, and micronutrients. It improves soil structure, water holding capacity, and microbial activity when applied to crops. Studies have shown that application of sericulture waste vermicompost enhances the yield and quality of mulberry leaves, thereby increasing silkworm cocoon production.

Biogas Production from Sericulture Waste

Sericulture waste, particularly silkworm litter and pupae, can be used as a feedstock for biogas production through anaerobic digestion. The process involves the following steps:

1. Waste collection and pre-treatment: Silkworm litter and pupae are collected and ground or pulverized to increase the surface area for microbial action. The waste may be mixed with water to achieve the desired solids content (8-10%) for optimal digestion.

2. Anaerobic digestion: The pre-treated waste is fed into an anaerobic digester, which is a sealed container maintained at mesophilic (35-40°C) or thermophilic (50-60°C) conditions. The digester is inoculated with anaerobic bacteria that break down the organic matter into biogas (a mixture of methane and carbon dioxide) and digestate (a nutrient-rich slurry).

3. Biogas collection and utilization: The biogas produced is collected in a gas holder and can be used for cooking, lighting, or electricity generation through a biogas engine. The digestate can be used as a liquid fertilizer or further processed into solid manure.

Studies have shown that silkworm litter alone can produce 300-600 L of biogas per kg of volatile solids, with a methane content of 50-70%. Silkworm pupae have a higher biogas potential of 800-1000 L per kg volatile solids due to their high lipid content. Co-digestion of silkworm litter with cattle manure or other agricultural wastes can enhance the biogas yield and stability of the digestion process.

A small-scale sericulture farm generating 1 ton of silkworm litter per year can produce enough biogas to meet the cooking needs of a family of 4-5 members. The biogas production from sericulture waste not only provides a clean and renewable energy source but also reduces the environmental pollution and greenhouse gas emissions associated with waste disposal.

Vermicomposting and biogas production are two eco-friendly and economically viable methods of converting sericulture waste into value-added products. These technologies not only help in waste management but also provide additional income and energy security to sericulture farmers. Proper training, infrastructure, and policy support are needed to promote the adoption of these technologies by the sericulture industry for sustainable and inclusive growth.

Chapter 15

Sericulture and Climate Change

Impact of climate change on mulberry and silkworm

Climate change, characterized by increasing temperatures, altered rainfall patterns, and more frequent extreme weather events, is having a significant impact on the sericulture industry. Mulberry, the sole food plant of the silkworm *Bombyx mori*, and the silkworm itself are both highly sensitive to changes in temperature and humidity. The effects of climate change on these two key components of sericulture are discussed below:

Impact on Mulberry

1. Leaf yield and quality:

- Increasing temperatures and drought stress can reduce mulberry leaf yield and quality. Studies have shown that leaf yield decreases by 10-30% under moisture stress conditions.

- High temperatures (above 40°C) during summer can cause scorching and drying of leaves, making them unsuitable for silkworm rearing.

- Altered rainfall patterns, with prolonged dry spells or heavy downpours, can affect leaf production and quality.

2. Nutrient content:

- Elevated CO2 levels can increase the C:N ratio in mulberry leaves, reducing their protein content and nutritional quality for silkworms.

- Drought stress can also alter the leaf biochemistry, affecting the levels of essential nutrients like amino acids and sugars.

3. Pest and disease incidence:

- Climate change can influence the population dynamics and geographical distribution of mulberry pests and diseases.

- Higher temperatures and humidity can favor the growth and spread of fungal diseases like powdery mildew and leaf spot.

- Insect pests like thrips, mealybugs, and whiteflies may become more prevalent and damaging under warmer conditions.

4. Soil health and fertility:

- Increased soil temperature and moisture stress can affect soil microbial activity and nutrient cycling in mulberry plantations.

- Soil organic carbon, a key determinant of soil health, may decline under climate change, impacting mulberry growth and productivity.

Impact on Silkworm

1. Larval growth and development:

- Silkworms are poikilothermic, meaning their body temperature varies with the environment. Optimal temperature for silkworm rearing is 24-28°C.

- Higher temperatures (above 30°C) can accelerate larval development, leading to reduced larval duration, cocoon weight, and silk quality.

- Lower temperatures (below 20°C) can slow down larval growth, prolong the larval period, and increase the risk of disease.

2. Cocoon yield and quality:

- High temperature and low humidity during late larval stages can reduce cocoon weight, shell weight, and silk filament length.

- Cocoon quality parameters like silk ratio, filament denier, and reelability are adversely affected by suboptimal rearing conditions.

3. Reproductive performance:

- High temperature and humidity during pupal and adult stages can negatively impact moth emergence, mating, and egg production.

- Reduced fecundity and fertility of silkmoths can affect the availability of quality silkworm eggs for subsequent rearing.

4. Disease incidence:

- Silkworms are susceptible to viral, bacterial, and fungal diseases, which can cause significant crop losses.

- High temperature and humidity favor the growth and transmission of pathogens like BmNPV (viral), BmIFV (viral), and Beauveria bassiana (fungal).

- Climate change can alter the host-pathogen interactions and disease dynamics in silkworm rearing.

Climate change poses significant challenges to the sericulture industry by affecting both mulberry and silkworm. Rising temperatures, altered rainfall, and increased frequency of extreme events can reduce leaf yield and quality, impair silkworm growth and development, and increase the incidence of pests and diseases. Developing climate-resilient mulberry varieties, improved silkworm breeds, and adaptive rearing practices are crucial for sustaining sericulture production under changing climatic conditions. Research, extension, and policy support are needed to enhance the resilience of sericulture farmers and ensure the long-term viability of this important agro-industry.

Strategies for climate resilient sericulture practices

Climate change, characterized by rising temperatures, altered rainfall patterns, and increased frequency of extreme weather events, poses significant challenges to the sericulture industry. Mulberry, the sole food plant of the silkworm *Bombyx mori,* and the silkworm itself are highly sensitive to changes in temperature and humidity. To ensure sustainable sericulture production under changing climatic conditions, it is essential to adopt climate resilient practices. Some key strategies are discussed below:

Breeding Climate Resilient Mulberry Varieties

Developing mulberry varieties that can withstand abiotic stresses like drought, heat, and salinity is crucial for climate resilient sericulture. Some approaches include:

- Screening and selection of mulberry genotypes with higher tolerance to temperature and moisture stress. Traits like deep root system, thick leaves, and efficient water use can be targeted.

- Hybridization and genetic engineering to develop mulberry varieties with improved stress tolerance. Genes for stress responsive proteins, osmolytes, and antioxidants can be incorporated.

- Evaluation and promotion of stress tolerant mulberry varieties in different agro-climatic zones for wider adaptability.

Improving Silkworm Breeds and Hybrids

Developing silkworm breeds and hybrids that can tolerate a wider range of temperature and humidity is essential for climate resilience. Some strategies are:

- Screening and selection of silkworm genotypes with higher tolerance to high temperature and low humidity conditions. Traits like shorter larval duration, higher survival rate, and better cocoon quality can be focused.

- Hybridization and marker-assisted selection to develop silkworm breeds with improved stress tolerance and disease resistance.

- Evaluation and promotion of climate resilient silkworm breeds and hybrids in different sericulture regions for better adaptability.

Modifying Rearing Practices

Adjusting the silkworm rearing practices according to the changing climatic conditions can help in mitigating the adverse effects. Some modifications include:

- Adjusting the rearing schedule to avoid peak summer temperatures and low humidity periods. Early or late season rearing can be adopted based on the regional conditions.

- Providing adequate ventilation, temperature control, and humidity management in the rearing houses. Use of evaporative cooling, fans, and humidifiers can help in maintaining optimal conditions.

- Adopting shoot rearing method, where silkworms are fed with whole shoots instead of harvested leaves. This reduces the leaf quality deterioration during transportation and storage.

- Using improved rearing trays and racks that allow better air circulation and hygiene. Plastic and bamboo trays with proper spacing can be used.

Integrated Pest and Disease Management

Climate change can influence the population dynamics and distribution of mulberry pests and silkworm diseases.

Integrated pest and disease management strategies are needed for climate resilience:

- Regular monitoring and surveillance of mulberry pests and diseases using field scouting, pheromone traps, and weather-based forewarning systems.

- Adoption of cultural practices like pruning, field sanitation, and intercropping to reduce pest and disease incidence.

- Use of bio-control agents like predators, parasitoids, and microbial pesticides for eco-friendly pest suppression.

- Timely application of need-based chemical pesticides with proper safety measures.

- Strict hygiene and disinfection practices in silkworm rearing to prevent the spread of diseases. Use of bed disinfectants, proper disposal of diseased larvae, and quarantine measures are important.

Soil and Water Conservation

Maintaining soil health and optimizing water use efficiency are crucial for climate resilient mulberry cultivation. Some practices include:

- Adoption of soil and water conservation measures like contour bunding, terracing, and mulching to reduce soil erosion and moisture loss.

- Incorporation of organic manures, green manures, and crop residues to improve soil organic carbon content and water holding capacity.

- Judicious use of irrigation water through drip and sprinkler systems. Scheduling irrigation based on crop growth stage and soil moisture status.

- Rainwater harvesting and efficient use of harvested water for critical irrigation.

Diversification and Risk Management

Diversifying the sericulture systems and adopting risk management strategies can enhance climate resilience. Some approaches are:

- Integration of sericulture with other compatible farming systems like horticulture, apiculture, and mushroom cultivation for income stability.

- Adoption of multi-tier mulberry cultivation with intercrops for efficient utilization of resources and risk spreading.

- Promotion of agro-forestry systems with mulberry as a component for ecological and economic benefits.

- Encouraging the rearing of different silkworm species (mulberry, tasar, eri, muga) and breeds to reduce the risk of crop failure.

- Crop insurance and weather-based insurance schemes to compensate for the losses due to climate extremes.

Capacity Building and Knowledge Management

Enhancing the adaptive capacity of sericulture farmers through capacity building and knowledge management is essential for climate resilience. Some strategies include:

- Training and skill development of farmers on climate resilient sericulture practices through demonstrations, exposure visits, and workshops.

- Strengthening the extension system for timely dissemination of weather advisories, pest and disease alerts, and management practices.

- Promoting farmer-to-farmer learning and community-based adaptation through field schools, study circles, and self-help groups.

- Documentation and sharing of traditional knowledge and innovative practices on climate resilient sericulture.

- Developing ICT-based decision support systems and mobile apps for providing real-time information on weather, markets, and management practices.

Adopting a combination of strategies like breeding climate resilient varieties, modifying rearing practices, integrated pest and disease management, soil and water conservation, diversification, and capacity building can help in developing climate resilient sericulture systems. These strategies need to be tailored to the specific agro-climatic conditions and socio-economic contexts of the sericulture regions. Collaborative efforts of researchers, extension workers, farmers, and policymakers are essential for the successful implementation of these strategies. With the right interventions and enabling policies, sericulture can continue to be a sustainable and profitable livelihood option for millions of farmers even under the changing climatic conditions.

Carbon sequestration potential of mulberry plantations

Mulberry (Morus spp.) is a fast-growing, deciduous tree that is widely cultivated for sericulture, as well as for its edible fruits, timber, and ecological benefits. In recent years, mulberry has gained attention for its potential to sequester atmospheric carbon dioxide (CO_2) and mitigate climate change. The carbon sequestration potential of mulberry plantations depends on various factors such as the cultivation practices, soil type, climate, and tree biomass production.

Carbon Sequestration in Mulberry Biomass

Mulberry trees have a high biomass production potential due to their fast growth rate and ability to regenerate after pruning. The carbon sequestered in the mulberry biomass is derived from the atmospheric CO_2 absorbed through photosynthesis. Studies have shown that mulberry plantations can accumulate significant amounts of carbon in their above-ground and below-ground biomass.

- A study in China found that the total carbon storage in mulberry trees (including roots, stems, branches, and leaves) ranged from 5.6 to 7.8 tons per hectare per year, depending on the planting density and management practices.

- Another study in India estimated that a one-hectare mulberry plantation with 13,600 plants could sequester about 8.9 tons of carbon per year in its biomass.

- The carbon sequestration potential of mulberry is higher than that of many other tree species due to its high leaf biomass production. Mulberry leaves have a strong ability to absorb air pollutants like CO2, carbon monoxide, and sulfur dioxide.

Carbon Sequestration in Soil

Apart from the biomass carbon, mulberry plantations also contribute to soil carbon sequestration through leaf litter decomposition and root turnover. Mulberry cultivation practices like reduced tillage, organic mulching, and intercropping can enhance soil organic carbon (SOC) stocks.

- A study in India found that the SOC content in mulberry fields ranged from 0.35% to 0.45% in the top 15 cm soil layer, depending on the cultivation practices. Mulberry fields with reduced tillage and organic mulching had higher SOC compared to conventional practices.

- Another study in China reported that the SOC stock in mulberry plantations increased by 18.5% after 20 years of cultivation, with an average annual increase of 0.92 tons per hectare.

- The addition of mulberry leaf litter and pruning residues to the soil enhances the SOC content and improves soil fertility. Mulberry litter has a low C:N ratio and decomposes quickly, releasing nutrients for plant uptake.

Factors Affecting Carbon Sequestration

The carbon sequestration potential of mulberry plantations varies depending on several factors:

1. Planting density: Higher planting density (up to 13,600 plants/ha) can increase the biomass carbon stock, but may reduce the leaf yield and quality.

2. Pruning and leaf harvest: Regular pruning and leaf harvesting for silkworm rearing can reduce the above-ground biomass carbon, but increase the leaf litter input to the soil.

3. Soil type and fertility: Mulberry grows well in deep, fertile, and well-drained soils. Soils with higher clay content and organic matter have higher carbon sequestration potential.

4. Climate and water availability: Mulberry is adapted to a wide range of climates, but grows best in warm and humid conditions with adequate water supply. Drought stress can reduce the biomass production and carbon sequestration.

5. Cultivation practices: Practices like reduced tillage, organic mulching, intercropping, and balanced fertilization can enhance the SOC stocks and improve the overall carbon sequestration potential of mulberry plantations.

Conclusion

Mulberry plantations have a significant potential for carbon sequestration, both in the tree biomass and soil. With proper management practices, one hectare of mulberry plantation can sequester about 8-10 tons of carbon per year, which is equivalent to offsetting the emissions from 2-3 cars. Promoting mulberry cultivation for sericulture and other uses can provide multiple ecological and economic benefits, including climate change mitigation, soil conservation, and sustainable livelihoods for farmers.

However, more research is needed to quantify the long-term carbon sequestration potential of mulberry under different agro-ecological conditions and management practices. Developing carbon accounting methodologies and incentive mechanisms for mulberry-based agroforestry systems can encourage farmers to adopt sustainable practices and contribute to global climate change mitigation efforts.

Chapter 16

Sericulture Extension and Training

Extension methods for technology dissemination in sericulture

Extension services play a crucial role in the dissemination of new technologies, improved practices, and innovations to sericulture farmers. Effective extension methods help in bridging the gap between research and field application, enhancing the adoption of sustainable practices, and improving the productivity and profitability of sericulture. Various extension methods are used for technology dissemination in sericulture, depending on the target audience, content, and resources available.

Farmer Field Schools (FFS)

Farmer Field Schools (FFS) are a participatory extension approach where a group of farmers (20-25) meet regularly in a field to learn about sericulture through hands-on experimentation and discovery-based learning. The key features of FFS are:

- Season-long learning: FFS covers the entire crop cycle from mulberry cultivation to silkworm rearing and cocoon production.

- Experiential learning: Farmers learn by doing and observing the results of their own experiments and practices.

- Facilitation by experts: Trained facilitators (extension workers or progressive farmers) guide the learning process and encourage farmer participation.

- Agro-ecosystem analysis: Farmers learn to observe and analyze the interactions between mulberry, silkworm, and the environment to make informed decisions.

- Group dynamics: FFS promotes collective learning, problem-solving, and decision-making among farmers.

FFS has been successfully used for promoting integrated pest management (IPM), soil health management, and improved silkworm rearing practices among sericulture farmers.

Demonstrations

Demonstrations are an effective extension method for showcasing the performance and benefits of new technologies or practices in a real-life setting. The types of demonstrations used in sericulture are:

- Method demonstration: It involves demonstrating a specific technique or skill, such as pruning, leaf harvest, or silkworm brushing, to a group of farmers.

- Result demonstration: It involves comparing the performance of a new technology or practice with the conventional method over a crop season, such as high-yielding mulberry variety vs. local variety.

- Field day: It is a one-day event where farmers visit a demonstration plot or a progressive farmer's field to observe and learn about the new technology or practice.

Demonstrations are usually conducted by extension workers or trained farmers in collaboration with research institutes or input suppliers. They help in creating awareness, building confidence, and facilitating the adoption of new technologies among farmers.

Training and Workshops

Training and workshops are organized to provide in-depth knowledge and skills on specific topics related to sericulture. The types of training and workshops are:

- Farmer training: It involves training farmers on various aspects of sericulture, such as mulberry cultivation, silkworm rearing, disease management, and post-cocoon processing. The training may be residential or non-residential, depending on the duration and content.

- Trainer's training: It involves training extension workers, para-extension workers, or progressive farmers to become trainers or master trainers. They, in turn, train other farmers in their respective areas.

- Workshops and seminars: These are organized to discuss specific issues, share experiences, or develop action plans related to sericulture development. They may involve farmers, researchers, extension workers, and other stakeholders.

Training and workshops are usually conducted by subject matter specialists from research institutes, universities, or government departments. They help in building the capacity of farmers and extension workers to adopt and promote new technologies.

Information and Communication Technology (ICT)

ICT tools are increasingly being used for technology dissemination in sericulture. Some of the ICT methods are:

- Mobile apps: Mobile apps are developed to provide information on mulberry cultivation, silkworm rearing, disease diagnosis, and market prices to farmers. They also facilitate two-way communication between farmers and experts.

- Videos and animations: Short videos and animations are created to demonstrate the steps involved in various sericulture practices. They are shared through social media, messaging apps, or local cable networks.

- Expert systems: Computer-based expert systems are developed to provide diagnostic and advisory services to farmers on mulberry and silkworm crop management.

- Tele-extension: It involves the use of telephone, video conferencing, or online platforms to provide real-time advice and solutions to farmers' queries and problems.

ICT methods help in reaching a large number of farmers quickly and cost-effectively. They also enable personalized and demand-driven extension services.

Farmer-to-Farmer Extension

Farmer-to-farmer extension involves the sharing of knowledge, skills, and experiences among farmers themselves. It is based on the premise that farmers are more likely to adopt new technologies or practices if they see them being successfully used by their peers. Some of the farmer-to-farmer extension methods are:

- Farmer field schools: As mentioned earlier, FFS promotes farmer-to-farmer learning and sharing of experiences.

- Farmer clubs: Farmer clubs are informal groups of farmers who meet regularly to discuss and learn about sericulture. They are facilitated by extension workers or progressive farmers.

- Farmer field days: Farmer field days are organized by progressive farmers to showcase their successful practices and innovations to other farmers.

- Farmer exchange visits: Farmers are taken on exposure visits to other sericulture areas or research stations to learn from their peers and experts.

Farmer-to-farmer extension helps in building social capital, local ownership, and sustainability of sericulture development efforts.

Print and Mass Media

Print and mass media are used to create awareness and disseminate information on sericulture to a wider audience. Some of the methods are:

- Leaflets and brochures: These are short, illustrated publications that provide information on specific topics related to sericulture. They are distributed to farmers through extension workers or input dealers.

- Posters and wall paintings: These are visual aids that convey key messages or practices related to sericulture. They are displayed in public places or on the walls of village buildings.

- Newspapers and magazines: Articles on sericulture technologies and success stories are published in local newspapers and magazines to reach a wider readership.

- Radio and television: Programs on sericulture are broadcast on local radio and television channels to create awareness and interest among farmers.

Print and mass media help in creating a conducive environment for the adoption of new technologies and practices in sericulture.

A combination of different extension methods is needed for effective technology dissemination in sericulture. The choice of methods depends on the local context, available resources, and the stage of technology adoption. Participatory and demand-driven approaches, such as farmer field schools and ICT-based methods, are gaining popularity due to their effectiveness in promoting sustainable sericulture practices. Extension services need to be continuously strengthened and adapted to the changing needs and aspirations of sericulture farmers.

Capacity building and skill development programs for sericulturists

Capacity building and skill development are crucial for the growth and sustainability of the sericulture industry. These programs aim to enhance the knowledge, skills, and competencies of sericulturists, enabling them to adopt best practices, improve productivity, and increase their income. Various organizations, including the Central Silk Board (CSB), state sericulture departments, and research institutes, conduct a range of capacity building and skill development programs for sericulturists.

Types of Programs

1. Skill Training & Enterprise Development Programmes (STEP):

- CSB conducts short-term training modules focusing on entrepreneurship development, in-house resource development, specialized overseas training, popularization of sericulture technologies, lab to land technology demonstration, and training impact assessment surveys.

- Popular programs under STEP include Resource Development Programme, Trainers Training Programme, Technology Upgradation Programme, and Management Development Programme.

2. Establishment of Sericulture Resource Centres (SRCs):

- SRCs are training cum facilitation centers established in select mulberry bivoltine and vanya silk clusters.

- They serve as a link between extension centers of R&D labs and beneficiaries, providing technology demonstration, skill enhancement, input supply, doubt clarification, and problem resolution at the cluster level.

- SRCs are managed by lead farmers, not-for-profit organizations, or sericulture societies for the benefit of cluster farmers.

3. Capacity Building & Training by R&D Institutes of CSB:

- CSB's R&D institutes conduct structured long-term training programs like Post Graduate Diploma in Sericulture.

- They also offer technology-based training for farmers and other stakeholders, and organize Krishi Melas, Farmer's Day, and farmer's interaction workshops to empower farmers and industry stakeholders.

4. Capacity Building in Seed Sector:

- Silkworm seed is a critical sector that drives the entire silk value chain. Therefore, capacity building and training in this sector are of paramount importance.

- CSB organizations managing different seed sub-sectors (mulberry, eri, tasar, and muga) conduct training programs for private silkworm seed producers, adopted seed rearers, managers, and workforce attached to government-owned grainages.

- The duration of these training programs varies from 1-4 weeks, depending on the training needs.

5. Vocational Training Programmes:

- Vocational training programs are conducted for rural youth in sericulture for their capacity building and employment generation.

- These programs focus on various aspects of sericulture, such as mulberry cultivation, silkworm rearing, silk reeling, and value addition.

- The duration of these programs ranges from a few weeks to several months, depending on the depth and complexity of the training.

Evaluation and Impact Assessment

Regular evaluation and impact assessment of training programs are essential to ensure their effectiveness and relevance. Some of the methods used for evaluation and impact assessment are:

- Pre and post-training assessments to measure the knowledge and skill gain of participants

- Feedback surveys to gather participants' opinions on the quality and usefulness of the training

- Field visits and follow-up surveys to assess the adoption of technologies and practices by trained sericulturists

- Impact studies to measure the socio-economic benefits of training programs, such as increased productivity, income, and employment generation

Studies have shown that capacity building and skill development programs have a positive impact on the knowledge, attitudes, and practices of sericulturists. Trained farmers have reported higher adoption of improved technologies, better disease management, and increased cocoon productivity compared to untrained farmers. Extension personnel who underwent training have shown improved communication skills, problem-solving abilities, and job satisfaction.

Challenges and Way Forward

Despite the efforts of various organizations, there are still some challenges in the effective implementation of capacity building and skill development programs for sericulturists:

- Limited reach and coverage of training programs, especially in remote and tribal areas

- Inadequate infrastructure and resources for conducting training programs

- Lack of qualified trainers and subject matter specialists

- Language barriers and low literacy levels of some sericulturists

- Limited follow-up and handholding support after training programs

To address these challenges and improve the effectiveness of capacity building and skill development programs, the following measures are suggested:

- Increasing the number and frequency of training programs, especially in underserved areas

- Developing mobile training units and e-learning modules to reach remote locations

- Strengthening the infrastructure and resources of training centers and SRCs

- Conducting regular training of trainers (ToT) programs to enhance the skills of trainers

- Developing training materials and modules in local languages and using audio-visual aids

- Providing post-training support and linkages with input suppliers, markets, and financial institutions

- Encouraging farmer-to-farmer learning and experience sharing through farmer field schools and exposure visits

Capacity building and skill development programs are essential for the growth and sustainability of the sericulture industry. These programs help sericulturists to acquire new knowledge, skills, and competencies, leading to improved productivity, income, and livelihoods. However, there is a need for continuous improvement and innovation in the design and delivery of these programs to ensure their effectiveness and relevance. Collaborative efforts of government agencies, research institutes, NGOs, and private sector organizations are crucial for the success of capacity building and skill development initiatives in sericulture.

Role of NGOs and self-help groups in sericulture promotion

Non-governmental organizations (NGOs) and self-help groups (SHGs) play a vital role in promoting sericulture as a sustainable livelihood option for rural communities, especially women. They contribute to the development of the sericulture industry through various activities such as capacity building, technology dissemination, credit facilitation, market linkage, and policy advocacy.

Role of NGOs in Sericulture Promotion

NGOs have been actively involved in promoting sericulture in many developing countries, including India. Some of the key roles played by NGOs in sericulture promotion are:

1. Awareness creation and mobilization: NGOs create awareness among rural communities about the potential of sericulture as a viable income-generating activity. They mobilize farmers, especially women, to form self-help groups and take up sericulture.

2. Capacity building and training: NGOs provide technical training to farmers on various aspects of sericulture, such as mulberry cultivation, silkworm rearing, disease management, and post-cocoon processing. They also organize exposure visits and demonstrations to promote the adoption of improved technologies and best practices.

3. Credit and input supply: NGOs facilitate access to credit for sericulture farmers through linkages with banks and microfinance institutions. They also help in the procurement and distribution of quality inputs like silkworm eggs, mulberry saplings, and rearing equipment.

4. Market linkage and value addition: NGOs assist sericulture farmers in marketing their produce by linking them with reelers, weavers, and other stakeholders in the silk value chain. They also promote value addition activities like silk reeling, spinning, and weaving to enhance the income of farmers.

5. Networking and policy advocacy: NGOs play a crucial role in building networks and alliances among sericulture stakeholders, including farmers, researchers, government agencies, and the private sector. They also engage in policy advocacy to create an enabling environment for the growth of the sericulture industry.

Some successful examples of NGO interventions in sericulture promotion include the BAIF Development Research Foundation in India, which has promoted tasar sericulture among tribal communities, and the Bangladesh Rural Advancement Committee (BRAC), which has integrated sericulture with its poverty alleviation programs.

Role of Self-Help Groups in Sericulture Promotion

Self-help groups (SHGs) are voluntary associations of 10-20 members, usually women, who come together to address common problems and promote collective action. SHGs have emerged as a powerful tool for the socio-economic empowerment of rural women and have played a significant role in promoting sericulture. Some of the key roles of SHGs in sericulture promotion are:

1. Collective production and marketing: SHGs enable small-scale sericulture farmers to achieve economies of scale through collective production and marketing of cocoons and silk. They help in reducing the cost of inputs, improving the bargaining power of farmers, and ensuring better prices for their produce.

2. Savings and credit mobilization: SHGs promote the habit of regular savings among members and provide them with access to credit for sericulture activities. They also help in linking SHGs with banks and other financial institutions for availing loans and subsidies.

3. Skill development and technology adoption: SHGs facilitate the training and skill development of members in various aspects of sericulture. They also promote the adoption of improved technologies and best practices through peer learning and group demonstrations.

4. Social empowerment and collective action: SHGs provide a platform for women to come together, share their experiences, and address common issues. They help in building the confidence and leadership skills of women and enable them to participate in decision-making processes at the household and community levels.

5. Convergence with government schemes: SHGs act as a bridge between sericulture farmers and government agencies implementing various schemes and programs for the development of the industry. They help in the identification of beneficiaries, distribution of subsidies, and monitoring of scheme implementation.

Some successful examples of SHG interventions in sericulture promotion include the Andhra Pradesh Rural Poverty Reduction Project, which has promoted sericulture through women SHGs, and the Mahila Kisan Sashaktikaran Pariyojana (MKSP) in India, which has integrated sericulture with its women empowerment programs.

NGOs and SHGs play a crucial role in promoting sericulture as a sustainable livelihood option for rural communities. They contribute to the development of the industry through various activities such as awareness creation, capacity building, credit facilitation, market linkage, and policy advocacy. The success of sericulture promotion depends on the effective collaboration and convergence among NGOs, SHGs, government agencies, and other stakeholders in the silk value chain. Strengthening the capacities of NGOs and SHGs and creating an enabling policy environment are essential for realizing the full potential of sericulture in poverty alleviation and women's empowerment.

Chapter 17

Sericulture Research and Innovations

Current research trends in mulberry and silkworm improvement

Mulberry and silkworm are the two key components of sericulture, the production of silk. In recent years, there has been significant research interest in improving both mulberry and silkworm to enhance silk productivity, quality, and sustainability. The current research trends focus on various aspects such as breeding, biotechnology, nutrition, physiology, and novel applications. Let's discuss these trends in detail:

Mulberry Improvement

1. Breeding for high-yielding and stress-tolerant varieties:

- Conventional breeding through hybridization and selection is being used to develop mulberry varieties with higher leaf yield, nutritional quality, and resistance to biotic and abiotic stresses.

- Molecular markers like SSRs and SNPs are being employed for marker-assisted selection and genetic diversity analysis of mulberry germplasm.

2. Genetic engineering for enhanced traits:

- Transgenic mulberry plants are being developed with genes for resistance to pests, diseases, drought, and salinity.

- Genes for improving leaf quality traits like protein content and antioxidant levels are also being introduced into mulberry.

3. Micropropagation and tissue culture:

- Efficient protocols for in vitro propagation of elite mulberry genotypes are being standardized for rapid multiplication and conservation of germplasm.

- Somatic embryogenesis and synthetic seed technology are being explored for mass propagation and long-term storage of mulberry.

4. Agroforestry and intercropping systems:

- Integration of mulberry with other compatible crops and trees is being studied for efficient land use, soil fertility management, and income diversification.

- Mulberry-based agroforestry systems are being designed for soil and water conservation, carbon sequestration, and ecosystem services.

5. Phytochemicals and nutraceuticals:

- Mulberry leaves, fruits, and bark are rich sources of bioactive compounds like flavonoids, anthocyanins, and alkaloids with antioxidant, anti-diabetic, and anti-inflammatory properties.

- Extraction, characterization, and utilization of these phytochemicals for food, pharmaceutical, and cosmetic applications are active areas of research.

Silkworm Improvement

1. Breeding for high-yielding and disease-resistant strains:

- Conventional breeding methods like hybridization, backcrossing, and selection are being used to develop silkworm strains with higher cocoon yield, silk quality, and resistance to diseases like pebrine, flacherie, and grasserie.

- Molecular markers are being used for genetic analysis, trait mapping, and marker-assisted selection in silkworm breeding programs.

2. Transgenesis and genome editing:

- Transgenic silkworms are being developed with genes for enhanced silk production, disease resistance, and novel silk properties like color, strength, and elasticity.

- CRISPR/Cas9 and other genome editing tools are being employed for precise modification of silkworm genes to study their functions and improve traits of interest.

3. Nutrition and physiology:

- The effects of different mulberry varieties, artificial diets, and feeding regimes on silkworm growth, development, and cocoon production are being investigated.

- Studies on silkworm gut microbiome, immune system, and hormonal regulation are providing insights into their physiology and potential targets for improvement.

4. Seri-biotechnology and novel applications:

- Silkworms are being explored as bioreactors for the production of recombinant proteins, vaccines, and other high-value compounds in the silk glands.

- Silk fibroin and sericin are being used for various biomedical applications like tissue engineering, drug delivery, and wound healing due to their biocompatibility and unique properties.

5. Climate change adaptation:

- The impact of climate change on silkworm physiology, cocoon production, and silk quality is being studied.

- Breeding and rearing strategies for developing climate-resilient silkworm strains and minimizing the adverse effects of temperature and humidity fluctuations are being investigated.

In addition to these specific trends, there is also a growing emphasis on integrating modern technologies like genomics, proteomics, metabolomics, and bioinformatics for a holistic understanding of mulberry and silkworm biology. Collaborative research involving breeders, biotechnologists, agronomists, and sericulture experts is crucial for translating the research findings into practical applications.

Moreover, there is increasing recognition of the ecological, social, and economic dimensions of sericulture. Research on sustainable sericulture practices, value addition, market linkages, and policy support is gaining momentum to ensure the livelihood security of sericulture farmers and the long-term viability of the silk industry.

The current research trends in mulberry and silkworm improvement are diverse, innovative, and multidisciplinary. They aim to address the challenges and opportunities in sericulture through the application of modern science and technology. With concerted efforts and investments in research and development, sericulture has the potential to become a more productive, profitable, and sustainable agro-industry in the future.

Application of remote sensing and GIS in sericulture

Remote sensing (RS) and Geographic Information Systems (GIS) are powerful tools that have found wide applications in various fields, including agriculture and sericulture. These technologies provide valuable spatial and temporal data that can be used for mapping, monitoring, and managing sericulture resources. The application of RS and GIS in sericulture is gaining momentum due to their potential to improve the efficiency, productivity, and sustainability of silk production.

Mulberry Cultivation

1. Mapping and suitability analysis:

- RS data from satellites like Landsat, MODIS, and Sentinel are being used to map the current area under mulberry cultivation and identify suitable lands for future expansion.

- GIS-based multi-criteria analysis considering factors like soil type, topography, climate, and water availability is being used to assess the suitability of different regions for mulberry cultivation.

2. Crop health monitoring:

- High-resolution satellite imagery and drone-based remote sensing are being used to monitor the health and growth of mulberry plantations.

- Vegetation indices like NDVI (Normalized Difference Vegetation Index) and SAVI (Soil Adjusted Vegetation Index) are being derived from RS data to assess the leaf area, biomass, and nutrient status of mulberry crops.

3. Precision farming:

- RS and GIS are being integrated with precision farming techniques like variable rate fertilization, irrigation scheduling, and pest management to optimize the inputs and improve the yield and quality of mulberry leaves.

- Soil moisture and nutrient maps derived from RS data are being used to guide the site-specific application of water and fertilizers in mulberry fields.

4. Yield estimation:

- RS-based models are being developed to estimate the leaf yield of mulberry plantations at different growth stages.

- Integration of RS data with crop simulation models and ground-based observations is being used to improve the accuracy of yield predictions and support decision-making in mulberry cultivation.

Silkworm Rearing

1. Rearing environment monitoring:

- RS data from weather satellites and ground-based sensors are being used to monitor the temperature, humidity, and light conditions in silkworm rearing houses.

- GIS-based spatial analysis is being used to identify the optimal locations for establishing silkworm rearing facilities based on factors like climate, accessibility, and proximity to mulberry fields.

2. Disease surveillance:

- RS and GIS are being explored for the early detection and monitoring of silkworm diseases like pebrine, flacherie, and grasserie.

- Spectral signatures and thermal imagery from RS data are being analyzed to identify the infected silkworm populations and guide the targeted interventions for disease management.

3. Sericulture information system:

- Web-based GIS platforms are being developed to integrate and disseminate various types of sericulture data like silkworm breed, rearing practices, cocoon production, and market prices.

- These platforms enable the stakeholders to access, analyze, and share the information for better planning, coordination, and decision-making in silkworm rearing.

Silk Value Chain

1. Mapping of silk industries:

- GIS is being used to map the location, capacity, and connectivity of silk reeling, weaving, and processing units.

- Spatial analysis of the silk value chain is helping to identify the gaps, bottlenecks, and opportunities for improving the efficiency and competitiveness of the silk industry.

2. Market analysis and trade:

- RS and GIS are being used to monitor the global silk production, consumption, and trade patterns.

- Spatial analysis of the silk market trends, prices, and quality is helping to inform the strategies for product diversification, branding, and export promotion.

3. Traceability and certification:

- RS and GIS are being integrated with blockchain technology to enable the traceability and certification of silk products from farm to fabric.

- Geo-tagged information on the origin, quality, and sustainability of silk is being used to enhance the transparency, trust, and value addition in the silk supply chain.

Challenges and Way Forward

Despite the potential benefits, the application of RS and GIS in sericulture is still in its nascent stage. Some of the challenges include:

- Limited availability and accessibility of high-resolution RS data for small-scale sericulture farms

- Lack of technical expertise and infrastructure for processing and analyzing RS and GIS data

- High cost of RS and GIS software, hardware, and data products

- Limited awareness and adoption of RS and GIS among sericulture stakeholders

To harness the full potential of RS and GIS in sericulture, there is a need for:

- Collaborative research involving remote sensing experts, GIS professionals, and sericulture scientists to develop and validate the RS and GIS-based models and applications

- Capacity building and training of sericulture extension workers, farmers, and industry stakeholders on the use and interpretation of RS and GIS data

- Development of low-cost, user-friendly, and mobile-based RS and GIS tools and platforms for sericulture

- Integration of RS and GIS with other emerging technologies like IoT, AI, and big data analytics for precision sericulture

- Policy support and investments for the creation and maintenance of RS and GIS infrastructure for sericulture

The application of RS and GIS in sericulture has immense potential to revolutionize the way we map, monitor, and manage the mulberry and silkworm resources. These technologies can provide valuable insights into the spatial and temporal dynamics of sericulture and support the decision-making at various stages of the silk value chain. However, realizing the full potential of RS and GIS in sericulture requires a concerted effort from researchers, practitioners, and policymakers to overcome the challenges and create an enabling environment for their adoption and utilization.

Intellectual property rights and patents in sericulture

Intellectual property rights (IPRs) play a crucial role in the sericulture industry, as they provide legal protection for various innovations, inventions, and creations related to mulberry cultivation, silkworm rearing, and silk production. The primary forms of IPRs relevant to sericulture are patents, plant variety protection, and geographical indications.

Patents:

Patents are granted for inventions that are novel, non-obvious, and have industrial applicability. In the context of sericulture, patents can be obtained for various innovations, such as:

1. Mulberry varieties: New mulberry varieties with improved traits like higher leaf yield, disease resistance, or stress tolerance can be patented. These patented varieties can provide a competitive advantage to sericulture farmers and ensure a steady supply of high-quality mulberry leaves.

2. Silkworm breeds: Genetically modified or selectively bred silkworm breeds with desirable characteristics, such as increased silk production, disease resistance, or unique silk properties (e.g., colour, strength, or elasticity), can be patented.

3. Sericulture equipment and machinery: Innovative equipment and machinery used in mulberry cultivation, silkworm rearing, silk reeling, or other sericulture processes can be patented. Examples include automated rearing systems, cocoon harvesting machines, or silk reeling devices.

4. Sericulture processes and methods: Novel processes or methods related to mulberry cultivation, silkworm rearing, silk production, or silk processing can be patented. This could include new techniques for disease management, feeding regimes, or silk dyeing and finishing processes.

5. Silk-based products and applications: Inventions involving the use of silk or silk-derived materials in various products or applications, such as biomedical devices, cosmetics, or textiles, can be patented.

Patents in sericulture provide legal protection for the inventors or patent holders, allowing them to exclude others from making, using, or selling their patented inventions for a limited period (typically 20 years). This exclusivity encourages innovation and investment in research and development, as it enables the patent holders to recoup their investments and gain a competitive advantage in the market.

Plant Variety Protection:

In addition to patents, sericulture also benefits from plant variety protection (PVP) systems, which are designed specifically for the protection of new plant varieties. PVP grants exclusive rights to breeders of new, distinct, uniform, and stable plant varieties, including mulberry varieties.

PVP systems, such as the one established under the Protection of Plant Varieties and Farmers' Rights (PPV&FR) Act in India, provide legal protection for mulberry breeders and encourage the development of improved mulberry varieties with desirable traits for sericulture.

Geographical Indications:

Geographical indications (GIs) are another form of IPR that can be relevant to sericulture. GIs identify goods as originating from a specific geographical region, where the quality, reputation, or other characteristics of the goods are attributable to their geographical origin.

In the context of sericulture, GIs can be used to protect and promote silk products from specific regions known for their unique silk production techniques or silk varieties. For example, the Geographical Indication Registry in India has registered GIs for silk products like Pochampally Ikat, Kanchipuram Silk Saree, and Muga Silk from Assam.

GIs can help sericulture farmers and silk producers differentiate their products in the market, command premium prices, and protect the reputation and authenticity of their regional silk products.

Importance of IPRs in Sericulture:

IPRs play a vital role in the sericulture industry by:

1. Encouraging innovation and investment in research and development by providing legal protection and exclusivity.

2. Facilitating technology transfer and commercialization through licensing or assignment of IPRs.

3. Promoting the development of improved mulberry varieties, silkworm breeds, and silk production techniques.

4. Protecting the interests of sericulture farmers, breeders, and silk producers by preventing unauthorized use of their intellectual property.

5. Enhancing the competitiveness and market value of sericulture products through branding and differentiation.

6. Fostering public-private partnerships and collaborations in sericulture research and development.

However, it is essential to strike a balance between providing adequate IPR protection and ensuring access to genetic resources and traditional knowledge for further research and development. Mechanisms like compulsory licensing, research exemptions, and benefit-sharing provisions can help address these concerns and promote the sustainable development of the sericulture industry.

Intellectual property rights, particularly patents, plant variety protection, and geographical indications, play a crucial role in the sericulture industry by incentivizing innovation, protecting investments, and promoting the development of improved mulberry varieties, silkworm breeds, and silk production techniques. Effective management and utilization of IPRs can contribute to the growth and competitiveness of the sericulture sector while ensuring equitable access to genetic resources and traditional knowledge.

Chapter 18

Global Sericulture Scenario

Major silk producing countries and their production trends

Silk production is a labor-intensive and intricate process that involves the cultivation of mulberry trees, rearing of silkworms, and the extraction of silk fibers from cocoons. While several countries are engaged in silk production, a few nations stand out as major contributors to the global silk industry.

China

China is the world's largest producer and exporter of silk, accounting for over 50% of global silk production. The country has a long-standing tradition of sericulture, dating back thousands of years. Major silk-producing regions in China include Sichuan, Zhejiang, Jiangsu, and Guangdong provinces. However, China's silk production has experienced a declining trend in recent years due to factors such as rising labor costs, urbanization, and competition from synthetic fibers.

India

India is the second-largest producer of silk in the world, contributing around 40% to the global silk production. The country is known for producing a variety of silk types, including mulberry, tasar, muga, and eri. The states of Karnataka, Andhra Pradesh, West Bengal, and Assam are the major silk-producing regions in India. India's silk production has shown an increasing trend over the past decade, driven by government initiatives, technological advancements, and growing domestic and international demand.

Uzbekistan

Uzbekistan has emerged as a significant player in the global silk industry, ranking third in silk production. The country's favorable climate and abundant mulberry plantations have contributed to its success in sericulture. Uzbekistan's silk production has witnessed a substantial increase in recent years, driven by government support and investments in modernizing the silk industry.

Vietnam

Vietnam is another notable silk-producing country, ranking fourth globally. The country's silk industry is concentrated in the northern and central regions, with a focus on mulberry silk production. Vietnam's silk production has experienced steady growth, fueled by increasing domestic demand and exports to international markets.

Thailand

Thailand is known for its high-quality silk products, particularly its renowned Thai silk. The country's silk production is primarily concentrated in the northeastern and southern regions. While Thailand's silk production has fluctuated over the years, it remains an important contributor to the global silk market, catering to both domestic and international demand.

Brazil

Brazil has emerged as a significant silk producer in the Americas, ranking sixth globally. The country's silk industry is centered in the states of Paraná and São Paulo, where favorable climatic conditions and government support have facilitated the growth of sericulture. Brazil's silk production has shown an increasing trend, driven by the growing demand for sustainable and eco-friendly textiles.

While these countries are the major players in the global silk industry, several other nations, such as Iran, North Korea, and Bangladesh, also contribute to silk production on a smaller scale. The silk industry is influenced by various factors, including technological advancements, changing consumer preferences, environmental concerns, and government policies. As a result, the production trends in these countries may fluctuate over time, reflecting the dynamic nature of the global silk market.

	2011	2015	2018	2019	2022	
China	104,000	170,000	120,000	-	50,000	Declining production, but still the largest producer globally
India	23,060	28,708	35,468	35,516	36,500	Steadily increasing production, second largest producer
Uzbekistan	1,100	1,070	1,200	-	2,400	Significant increase in recent years
Vietnam	500	600	-	-	1,700	Substantial increase
Thailand	750	687	-	-	335	Declining production
Brazil	480	380	-	-	290	Declining production

Key points:

China remains the world's largest silk producer, but its production has declined substantially from over 100,000 metric tons in 2011 to around 50,000 metric tons in 2022.

India has seen a steady increase in silk production, becoming the second-largest producer globally, with around 36,500 metric tons produced in 2022.

Uzbekistan and Vietnam have experienced significant increases in silk production in recent years, with Uzbekistan producing around 2,400 metric tons and Vietnam producing 1,700 metric tons in 2022.

Thailand and Brazil have seen declining trends in silk production over the years.

Please note that the data may vary slightly across different sources, and the most recent years' data may not be available for all countries.

International trade and marketing of silk and silk products

Silk, a luxurious and highly coveted natural fiber, has played a significant role in international trade for centuries. The silk industry encompasses a wide range of products, from raw silk to finished goods such as fabrics, garments, and accessories. The global silk trade is driven by a combination of factors, including cultural traditions, fashion trends, and the demand for high-quality textiles.

Silk Production and Exporting Countries

China has long been the world's leading producer and exporter of silk, accounting for over 50% of global silk production. The country's sericulture industry is deeply rooted in its history and cultural heritage. Major silk-producing regions in China include Sichuan, Zhejiang, Jiangsu, and Guangdong provinces.

India is the second-largest producer of silk, contributing around 40% to the global silk production. The country is known for producing a variety of silk types, including mulberry, tasar, muga, and eri. The states of Karnataka, Andhra Pradesh, West Bengal, and Assam are the major silk-producing regions in India.

Other notable silk-producing countries include Uzbekistan, Vietnam, Thailand, and Brazil. These countries have established sericulture industries and contribute to the global silk trade.

Silk Importing Countries and Markets

The demand for silk products is global, with major importing countries spanning across various regions. Some of the key silk importing countries and markets include:

- United States: The United States is a significant importer of silk products, driven by the demand for luxury fashion and home furnishings.

- European Union: Countries like Italy, France, Germany, and the United Kingdom are major importers of silk, catering to the high-end fashion and textile industries.

- Japan: Japan has a long-standing tradition of silk production and consumption, with a strong demand for high-quality silk products.

- Middle East: Countries in the Middle East, such as the United Arab Emirates, Saudi Arabia, and Qatar, have a growing appetite for luxury silk products.

- Emerging Markets: Emerging economies like China, India, and Southeast Asian countries are witnessing an increasing demand for silk products due to rising disposable incomes and changing consumer preferences.

Marketing Strategies for Silk Products

The marketing of silk products often revolves around emphasizing the luxury, exclusivity, and cultural significance associated with silk. Common marketing strategies include:

1. Branding and Storytelling: Silk brands often leverage the rich history and cultural heritage of silk production to create compelling brand narratives and establish a sense of exclusivity.

2. Emphasizing Quality and Craftsmanship: Silk products are marketed as high-quality, meticulously crafted items, highlighting the skill and expertise involved in their production.

3. Sustainability and Ethical Sourcing: With increasing consumer awareness about sustainability, silk brands are highlighting their commitment to ethical and environmentally responsible practices in silk production.

4. Influencer Marketing and Celebrity Endorsements: Luxury silk brands often collaborate with influencers, celebrities, and fashion icons to promote their products and tap into aspirational consumer segments.

5. Experiential Marketing: Silk brands may create immersive experiences, such as pop-up stores, fashion shows, or exhibitions, to engage consumers and showcase the beauty and versatility of silk products.

6. Digital Marketing and E-commerce: With the rise of online shopping, silk brands are leveraging digital marketing channels, including social media, influencer collaborations, and e-commerce platforms, to reach a global audience.

The international trade and marketing of silk and silk products are driven by a combination of cultural traditions, luxury positioning, and evolving consumer preferences. As the demand for high-quality and sustainable products continues to grow, the silk industry is adapting its production and marketing strategies to cater to the changing global market landscape.

Challenges and opportunities for the global silk industry

The global silk industry faces several challenges that hinder its growth and sustainability, while also presenting opportunities for innovation and expansion.

Challenges:

Limited Supply and High Production Costs

Silk production is a labour-intensive and time-consuming process, involving the cultivation of mulberry trees, rearing of silkworms, and the extraction of silk fibers from cocoons. This labour-intensive nature, coupled with the limited availability of skilled workers, contributes to the high production costs associated with silk. Additionally, the supply of raw silk is limited, as the production process is heavily dependent on favorable climatic conditions and the availability of mulberry leaves.

Competition from Synthetic Fibers

The silk industry faces intense competition from synthetic fibers, such as polyester and nylon, which are often more affordable and easier to produce. These synthetic alternatives have gained popularity due to their durability, versatility, and lower production costs, posing a significant challenge to the silk industry's market share.

Environmental Concerns

The silk industry has been criticized for its environmental impact, particularly in terms of water consumption, energy usage, and the use of chemicals in the production process. Concerns over sustainability and eco-friendliness have led to increased scrutiny and pressure on the industry to adopt more environmentally responsible practices.

Fluctuating Prices and Market Volatility

The silk market is subject to price fluctuations and volatility due to various factors, such as changes in demand, variations in the cost of raw materials (e.g., mulberry leaves), and fluctuations in exchange rates. This volatility can create uncertainty and challenges for silk producers, traders, and manufacturers.

Ethical Concerns

The traditional silk production process involves the killing of silkworms by boiling or baking them, which has raised ethical concerns among consumers and animal rights activists. This has led to a growing demand for cruelty-free and ethical alternatives, such as "peace silk" or "Ahimsa silk," where the silkworms are allowed to emerge naturally from their cocoons.

Opportunities:

Growing Demand for Luxury and Sustainable Products

Despite the challenges, the silk industry presents significant opportunities due to the increasing demand for luxury and sustainable products. As consumer awareness and purchasing power grow, particularly in emerging markets, the demand for high-quality and eco-friendly silk products is expected to rise.

Product Diversification and Innovation

The silk industry has the potential to diversify its product offerings and explore new applications beyond traditional textiles. Silk-based biomaterials, for instance, are finding applications in the medical, cosmetic, and pharmaceutical industries, presenting new avenues for growth and innovation.

Technological Advancements

Advancements in sericulture practices, breeding techniques, and silk processing technologies offer opportunities for improved yields, quality, and sustainability. Innovations such as genetically modified silk materials, eco-friendly dyeing processes, and automation in silk production can enhance efficiency and reduce environmental impact.

Sustainable and Ethical Production

The growing demand for sustainable and ethical products presents an opportunity for the silk industry to adopt more environmentally responsible and cruelty-free practices. By embracing sustainable farming methods, implementing integrated pest management, and promoting ethical treatment of silkworms, the industry can cater to conscious consumers and differentiate itself in the market.

Global Trade and Collaboration

Initiatives such as the Belt and Road Initiative (BRI) and the Silk Road Economic Belt are fostering increased connectivity and collaboration between Asia, Europe, and Africa. These initiatives present opportunities for silk-producing countries to expand their export markets, strengthen trade relationships, and benefit from infrastructure development and economic cooperation.

Cultural Heritage and Tourism

The silk industry holds significant cultural and historical value, particularly in regions along the ancient Silk Road. By leveraging this cultural heritage and promoting silk-related tourism, the industry can generate additional revenue streams and contribute to the preservation of traditional silk-making techniques and cultural practices.

To capitalize on these opportunities and overcome the challenges, the global silk industry must embrace innovation, sustainability, and ethical practices. Collaboration among stakeholders, including governments, producers, researchers, and consumers, is crucial for driving positive change and ensuring the long-term viability and growth of the silk industry.

Chapter 19

Future Prospects of Sericulture

Diversification of sericulture products and value addition

Sericulture, the cultivation of silkworms for the production of silk, has traditionally been focused on the production of silk fibers for the textile industry. However, in recent years, there has been a growing interest in diversifying sericulture products and exploring value-addition opportunities to enhance the economic viability of the industry.

Silk Biomaterials

One of the most promising areas of diversification is the use of silk proteins, particularly fibroin and sericin, in the biomedical and pharmaceutical industries. These proteins possess unique properties, such as biocompatibility, biodegradability, and mechanical strength, making them suitable for various applications.

- Silk fibroin has been used in the development of scaffolds for tissue engineering, wound dressings, and drug delivery systems.

- Sericin, a protein traditionally discarded during silk processing, has found applications in cosmetics, nutraceuticals, and as an antioxidant and antimicrobial agent.

Sericulture By-products

Sericulture generates a significant amount of by-products and waste, which can be transformed into valuable products through proper processing and value addition.

- Silkworm pupae: Rich in proteins, fats, and minerals, silkworm pupae can be utilized as animal feed, in the production of pharmaceuticals, and as a source of chitin and chitosan for various applications.

- Silkworm feces (litter): Traditionally used as fertilizer, silkworm litter can also be processed to extract valuable compounds like solanesol, a precursor for cardiac drugs, and chlorophyll, used in treating gastric disorders.

- Mulberry leaves and stem waste: These can be converted into organic fertilizers, animal feed, or used for the extraction of bioactive compounds with potential applications in the food, pharmaceutical, and cosmetic industries.

Non-textile Applications

Silk fibers and cocoons can be utilized in various non-textile applications, adding value to the sericulture industry.

- Handicrafts: Silk cocoons and waste silk can be used to create decorative items, such as garlands, flower vases, dolls, and jewelry, catering to the growing demand for eco-friendly and sustainable products.

- Paper and packaging: Silk fibers can be processed into high-quality paper and packaging materials, leveraging their strength and durability.

- Biocomposites: Silk fibers can be incorporated into biocomposites, enhancing their mechanical properties and biodegradability, with applications in the automotive, construction, and consumer goods industries.

Value Addition through Processing

Value addition can also be achieved through the processing and transformation of silk products.

- Silk yarn and fabric dyeing: Exploring natural dyes and eco-friendly dyeing techniques can cater to the growing demand for sustainable and environmentally friendly textile products.

- Silk fabric finishing: Specialized finishing techniques, such as enzyme treatments or plasma treatments, can impart unique properties to silk fabrics, increasing their value and expanding their applications.

- Silk blends: Blending silk with other natural or synthetic fibers can create innovative textile products with tailored properties, catering to diverse market segments.

To fully realize the potential of diversification and value addition in sericulture, collaborative efforts among researchers, industry stakeholders, and policymakers are crucial. This includes investing in research and development, promoting sustainable practices, and creating awareness about the versatility and value of sericulture products beyond traditional silk textiles.

Integration of sericulture with other farming systems

Sericulture, the cultivation of silkworms for the production of silk, can be effectively integrated with various other farming systems to create a sustainable and diversified agricultural model. This integration not only optimizes resource utilization but also enhances overall productivity, profitability, and environmental sustainability.

Sericulture and Crop Cultivation

Sericulture can be seamlessly integrated with crop cultivation, particularly with the cultivation of mulberry, which serves as the primary food source for silkworms. The integration of sericulture with crop farming allows for efficient land utilization, as mulberry plantations can be established on field bunds, boundaries, or as intercropping systems. Additionally, the by-products from sericulture, such as silkworm litter and pupae, can be used as organic fertilizers, enhancing soil fertility and reducing the reliance on chemical fertilizers.

Sericulture and Livestock Farming

The integration of sericulture with livestock farming, such as dairy, poultry, or small ruminants, creates a symbiotic relationship where the waste from one system becomes a valuable input for the other. Livestock manure can be used as organic fertilizer for mulberry cultivation, while crop residues and by-products from sericulture can serve as animal feed. This closed-loop system promotes efficient nutrient cycling and reduces the need for external inputs.

Sericulture and Agroforestry

Agroforestry systems, which involve the cultivation of trees alongside agricultural crops or livestock, can be effectively integrated with sericulture. Mulberry plants can be grown as an understory crop in agroforestry systems, providing shade and shelter for silkworms while also contributing to soil conservation and biodiversity. Additionally, the leaf litter from trees can be used as a mulching material in mulberry plantations, improving soil moisture retention and nutrient availability.

Sericulture and Aquaculture

The integration of sericulture with aquaculture, such as fish farming or rice-fish systems, can create a sustainable and productive farming model. Silkworm litter and other organic waste from sericulture can be used as feed for fish, while the water from fish ponds can be utilized for irrigating mulberry plantations. This integration promotes efficient water management and nutrient recycling, reducing the need for external inputs.

Sericulture and Horticulture

Sericulture can be integrated with horticulture, where mulberry plantations can be established as border crops or intercropped with fruit trees or vegetable crops. This integration optimizes land use and provides additional sources of income from the sale of horticultural products. Furthermore, the by-products from sericulture can be used as organic fertilizers for horticultural crops, promoting sustainable and eco-friendly farming practices.

Sericulture and Apiculture

The integration of sericulture with apiculture (beekeeping) can be mutually beneficial. Mulberry plantations provide a rich source of nectar and pollen for honeybees, while the bees contribute to the pollination of mulberry flowers, enhancing fruit and seed production. Additionally, the honey produced can serve as an additional source of income for farmers, further diversifying their revenue streams.

The integration of sericulture with other farming systems not only enhances productivity and profitability but also promotes sustainable agricultural practices by optimizing resource utilization, reducing waste, and promoting nutrient cycling. This holistic approach to farming contributes to the overall well-being of rural communities, ensuring food security, economic stability, and environmental conservation.

Roadmap for sustainable growth of the sericulture industry

The sericulture industry plays a crucial role in providing livelihood opportunities, generating employment, and contributing to the economic development of rural communities. However, to ensure its long-term sustainability and growth, a comprehensive roadmap is necessary. This roadmap should address various aspects, including technological advancements, environmental considerations, market dynamics, and policy support.

Technological Advancements

Embracing technological innovations is essential for enhancing productivity, efficiency, and quality in the sericulture industry. Key areas for technological interventions include:

1. Developing high-yielding and disease-resistant mulberry varieties through advanced breeding techniques and biotechnology.

2. Implementing precision farming practices, such as soil nutrient management, irrigation optimization, and integrated pest management, to improve resource efficiency and reduce environmental impact.

3. Automating processes like silkworm rearing, cocoon harvesting, and silk reeling to increase productivity and reduce labor-intensive tasks.

4. Adopting digital technologies, including remote sensing, data analytics, and decision support systems, to aid in monitoring, forecasting, and decision-making processes.

Environmental Sustainability

Promoting environmentally sustainable practices is crucial for the long-term viability of the sericulture industry. Strategies to achieve this include:

1. Encouraging organic mulberry cultivation and adopting eco-friendly pest management techniques to reduce the use of chemical pesticides and fertilizers.

2. Implementing water conservation measures, such as drip irrigation and rainwater harvesting, to optimize water usage in mulberry cultivation.

3. Promoting the use of renewable energy sources, such as solar power, in sericulture operations to reduce the carbon footprint.

4. Developing effective waste management systems to recycle and reuse by-products from sericulture activities, such as silkworm litter and pupae.

Market Development and Diversification

Expanding market opportunities and diversifying product offerings are essential for the growth of the sericulture industry. Key strategies include:

1. Promoting the development of value-added silk products, such as silk-based biomaterials, cosmetics, and nutraceuticals, to tap into emerging markets.

2. Exploring new export markets and strengthening existing trade relationships through bilateral agreements and trade facilitation measures.

3. Enhancing product quality and standardization to meet international market demands and comply with global trade regulations.

4. Developing branding and marketing strategies to promote silk products, highlighting their unique qualities, cultural significance, and sustainability aspects.

Policy Support and Institutional Strengthening

Supportive policies and strong institutional frameworks are crucial for the sustainable growth of the sericulture industry. Key initiatives include:

1. Formulating comprehensive national and regional sericulture policies that address issues such as research and development, technology transfer, infrastructure development, and market support.

2. Strengthening extension services and capacity-building programs to equip farmers and industry stakeholders with the latest knowledge and skills.

3. Promoting public-private partnerships and encouraging private sector investment in sericulture-related

infrastructure, such as processing units and cold storage facilities.

4. Providing financial incentives, subsidies, and access to credit facilities to support farmers, entrepreneurs, and small-scale enterprises in the sericulture sector.

5. Fostering international collaborations and knowledge-sharing platforms to facilitate the exchange of best practices, research findings, and technological advancements.

By implementing a comprehensive roadmap that addresses technological advancements, environmental sustainability, market development, and policy support, the sericulture industry can achieve sustainable growth while contributing to economic development, employment generation, and environmental conservation.

Chapter 20

Glossary of Sericulture Terms

Compilation of commonly used technical terms in sericulture

Sericulture - The cultivation of silkworms for the production of raw silk.

Moriculture - The cultivation of mulberry plants, which serve as the food source for the silkworms.

Voltinism - It refers to the number of life cycles per year that a typical silkworm completes. Depending on the eco-race, a silkworm may be univoltine (one life cycle per year), bivoltine (two life cycles per year), or multivoltine (multiple life cycles per year).

Brushing - The process of transferring silkworm eggs or newly hatched larvae onto the rearing bed or tray.

Rearing - The process of raising silkworms from the egg stage to the cocoon stage, involving feeding them with mulberry leaves.

Cocoon - The protective shell spun by the silkworm larvae during the pupal stage, composed of silk filaments.

Stifling - The process of killing the silkworm pupae inside the cocoons, typically by exposing them to heat or chemicals, to prevent the emergence of adult moths and facilitate silk reeling.

Reeling - The process of unwinding the silk filaments from the cocoons to obtain raw silk.

Deflossing - The removal of the outer, loose fibers from the cocoon before reeling, to obtain a smooth and continuous silk filament.

Silk Waste - The by-product obtained during the reeling process, consisting of short, tangled fibers that cannot be reeled.

Spun Silk - Silk yarn produced by spinning the silk waste or short fibers, rather than reeling the continuous filaments from the cocoons.

Grainage - The process of obtaining silkworm eggs from the mated female moths, involving controlled environmental conditions to ensure the quality and viability of the eggs.

Seed Cocoons - Cocoons set aside for the purpose of obtaining eggs for the next generation of silkworms, rather than reeling them for silk production.

Apiculture - The rearing of honeybees for the production of honey and other bee products. Apiculture is often integrated with sericulture as bees help in pollinating mulberry flowers.

Chawki Rearing - The initial stage of silkworm rearing, involving the care and feeding of young larvae until they reach the desired age or size for further rearing.

Cocoon Cooking - The process of softening the sericin (natural gum) that binds the silk filaments in the cocoon, typically by immersing the cocoons in hot water or an alkaline solution, to facilitate silk reeling.

Denier - The unit used to measure the linear density or thickness of silk filament yarn, representing the weight in grams of 9,000 meters of the filament.

Litting - The process of transferring silkworm larvae from one rearing bed to another during different stages of their growth.

Mounting - The process of providing a suitable surface or support for the mature silkworms to spin their cocoons.

Nistari - The process of sorting and separating the good cocoons from the defective ones before reeling.

Piercing - The process of making a small hole in the cocoon to locate the end of the silk filament for reeling.

Stifling - The process of killing the silkworm pupae inside the cocoons, typically by exposing them to heat or chemicals, to prevent the emergence of adult moths and facilitate silk reeling.

Throwing - The process of combining and twisting together single silk filaments to form a thicker and stronger silk yarn.

Ahimsa Silk - Also known as "peace silk" or "vegetarian silk," it refers to the silk obtained without killing the silkworm pupae. The cocoons are allowed to emerge naturally, and the silk is harvested from the broken cocoon shells.

Batching - The process of sorting and grading silkworm eggs based on their quality, colour, and size before incubation.

Mr. Katta Subramanya Sai Teja is currently pursuing his Ph.D. at Dr. RPCAU, PUSA, Bihar in the Department of Entomology. He graduated from ANGRAU Bapatla in Andhra Pradesh. He received his M.Sc. from the Department of Agricultural Entomology at the University of Agricultural Sciences, GKVK, Bengaluru. He cleared ICAR-JRF 2019, Joint CSIR-UGC NET JRF 2021, and ASRB-NET 2023. He has published three research papers, two review papers, and 20 popular articles. He received the best M.Sc thesis award.

Ms. Sujatha G S, presently working in Food Corporation of India as a Technical Assistant (Quality Control) at Mysuru. She completed her Under Graduation from University of Agricultural Science Bengaluru, V C Farm Mandya in 2019. She has been qualified ICAR-Junior research fellowship (JRF) in 2019 and ICAR-NET in the year 2021.She completed her M.Sc. (Ag) in the Department of Entomology, Indian Agricultural Research Institute, New Delhi. She has been awarded with the Senior research fellowship (SRF) and joined as a Ph.D. Scholar at Dr. Rajendra Prasad Central Agricultural University, PUSA,

Bihar. She has been cleared AFO and FCI examination in 2023. She has published two research papers, 6 Book chapters, 10 popular articles. She has received the Excellence of Research award.

Ms. Dharanikota Lalithambica Devi, presently pursuing her Ph.D. from Govind Ballabh Pant University of Agriculture and Technology, Pantnagar, Uttarakhand in field of Agricultural Entomology. She had graduated with distinction from Agricultural college, Rajamahendravaram (ANGRAU). She had completed her master's in Entomology from Dr. RPCAU, PUSA, Bihar. She has qualified ICAR-NET in the year 2023 and also qualified SRF-2023.

Mr. G. Anil Kumar is a dedicated researcher currently doing his Ph.D. research at the Indian Institute of Maize Research, Winter Nursery Centre, Rajendranagar, Hyderabad. He obtained his Bachelor's degree from the Agricultural College, Rajamahendravaram, also under the esteemed Acharya NG Ranga Agricultural University, graduating with first-class honors and distinction. He completed his Master of Science in Agricultural Entomology from the University of Agricultural Sciences, GKVK, Bengaluru, with first-class honors and distinction. Currently pursuing his Ph.D. at the Agricultural College, Bapatla within the prestigious Acharya NG Ranga Agricultural University, located in Lam, Guntur, and Andhra Pradesh. He has cleared ICAR-JRF 2019, and ASRB-NET 2023. He has authored five research articles, three book chapters, and 10 engaging popular articles.